Litigating the Right to Health

Courts, Politics, and Justice in Indonesia

Policy Studies
an East-West Center series

Series Editors
Dieter Ernst and Marcus Mietzner

Description
Policy Studies presents original research on pressing economic and political policy challenges for governments and industry across Asia, and for the region's relations with the United States. Written for the policy and business communities, academics, journalists, and the informed public, the peer-reviewed publications in this series provide new policy insights and perspectives based on extensive fieldwork and rigorous scholarship.

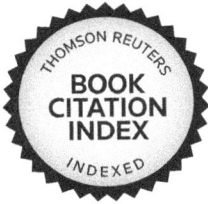

THOMSON REUTERS
BOOK CITATION INDEX
INDEXED

Policy Studies is indexed in the *Web of Science Book Citation Index*. The *Web of Science* is the largest and most comprehensive citation index available.

Notes to Contributors
Submissions may take the form of a proposal or complete manuscript. For more information on the Policy Studies series, please contact the Series Editors.

Editors, Policy Studies
East-West Center
1601 East-West Road
Honolulu, Hawai'i 96848-1601
Tel: 808.944.7197
Publications@EastWestCenter.org
EastWestCenter.org/PolicyStudies

Policy
Studies | 76

Litigating the Right to Health
Courts, Politics, and Justice in Indonesia

Andrew Rosser

Litigating the Right to Health: Courts, Politics, and Justice in Indonesia
Andrew Rosser

ISSN 1547-1349 (print) and 1547-1330 (electronic)
ISBN 978-0-86638-278-6 (print) and 978-0-86638-279-3 (electronic)

Print copies are available from Amazon.com. Free electronic copies of most titles are available on the East-West Center website, at EastWestCenter.org/PolicyStudies, where submission guidelines can also be found. Questions about the series should be directed to:

Publications Office
East-West Center
1601 East-West Road
Honolulu, Hawai'i 96848-1601

Telephone: 808.944.7197

EWCBooks@EastWestCenter.org
EastWestCenter.org/PolicyStudies

Cover: Elderly people associated with People Concerned About Health, a community group, protest against the privatization of three local government hospitals outside Jakarta City Hall in January 2006.

Photo credit: TEMPO/Arie Basuki.

Contents

List of Acronyms

ADB	Asian Development Bank
APINDO	Asosiasi Pengusaha Indonesia, Indonesian Employers Association
ASABRI	Asuransi Sosial Angkatan Bersenjata Republik Indonesia, social insurance for armed forces personnel, which provides pensions for military officials
ASKES	Asuransi Kesehatan untuk Pegawai Negeri Sipil dan Pensiunan TNI/POLRI, health insurance for civil servants and retired armed forces personnel
ASKESKIN	Asuransi Kesehatan Masyarakat Miskin, health insurance for the poor
ASKESOS	Asuransi Kesejahteraan Sosial, social welfare insurance
BLT	Bantuan Langsung Tunai, temporary direct cash assistance
BLU	badan layanan umum, public service bodies
BOS	Bantuan Operasional Sekolah, school operational assistance
BPJS	badan penyelenggara jaminan sosial, social security provider

BUMD	badan usaha milik daerah, regional state-owned enterprises
BUMN	badan usaha milik negara, central-government-owned SOEs
DKR	Dewan Kesehatan Rakyat, Peoples' Health Council
DPR	Dewan Perwakilan Rakyat, People's Representative Council, the national parliament
FITRA	Forum Indonesia untuk Transparansi Anggaran, Indonesian Forum for Budget Transparency
FRPK	Forum Rakyat Peduli Kesehatan, People Concerned About Health
ICW	Indonesia Corruption Watch
IDI	Ikatan Dokter Indonesia, Indonesian Doctors' Association
IHCS	Indonesian Human Rights Committee For Social Justice
INFID	Indonesian NGO Forum on Indonesian Development
Institut Hak Ekosob	Institute for Ecosoc Rights
JAMKESMAS	Jaminan Kesehatan Masyarakat, community health insurance
JAMSOSTEK	Jaminan Sosial Tenaga Kerja, social insurance for private-sector workers
JKN	Jaminan Kesehatan Nasional, mandatory national health insurance
JRKN	Jaringan Relawan Kemanusiaan untuk Nunukan, Volunteers' Humanitarian Network for Nunukan

KAJS	Komite Aksi Jaminan Sosial, Action Committee for Social Security
KuIS	Koalisi untuk Indonesia Sehat, Coalition for a Healthy Indonesia
LBH Kesehatan	Lembaga Bantuan Hukum Kesehatan, Health Legal Aid Institute
MPR	Majelis Permusyawaratan Rakyat, People's Consultative Assembly, Indonesia's highest legislative body
NGO	non-governmental organization
PDI-P	Partai Demokrasi Indonesia-Perjuangan, Indonesian Democratic Party of Struggle
perjan	a type of state-owned enterprise that is wholly government owned, concerned with the public good, and not-for-profit in orientation
PNPM	Program Nasional Pemberdayaan Masyarakat, community empowerment program
Prakarsa	Welfare Initiative for Better Societies
PTs	perseroan terbatas, limited liability companies
PTUN	pengadilan tata usaha negara, state administrative court
RASKIN	Beras Untuk Keluarga Miskin, rice subsidy for poor families
RSUD	Rumah Sakit Umum Daerah, public hospitals owned and run by provincial or district governments
RSUP	Rumah Sakit Umum Pemerintah, public hospitals owned and run by the central government
RTU	regional technical unit
SOE	state-owned enterprise

SRMI	Serikat Rakyat Miskin Indonesia, Indonesian Poor Peoples' League
TASPEN	Tabungan dan Asuransi Pegawai Negeri, pensions for civil servants
TURC	Trade Union Rights Centre
UDHR	Universal Declaration of Human Rights
UNICEF	United Nations Children's Fund
Unit Swadana	self-financing bureaucratic unit
UPT	unit pelaksana teknis, technical implementation unit
WHO	World Health Organization
YLBHI	Yayasan Lembaga Bantuan Hukum Indonesia, Indonesian Legal Aid Foundation
YLKI	Yayasan Lembaga Konsumen Indonesia, Indonesian Consumers Foundation
YLPKKI	Yayasan Lembaga Pemberdayaan Konsumen Kesehatan Indonesia, Indonesian Health Consumers Empowerment Foundation

Executive Summary

In recent years there has been a dramatic increase in health rights litigation in low- and middle-income countries, triggering debate about the effects of such litigation in terms of the equity and effectiveness of health systems in these countries.

On one side of this debate, proponents of rights-based approaches to health have argued that such litigation can be an effective way of promoting the fulfilment of health rights in practice because it enables citizens to hold governments accountable for policies or bureaucratic decisions that breach these rights.

On the other side, critics of such approaches have claimed that health rights litigation is more readily employed by middle-class citizens than the poor, leading to regressive effects in terms of the allocation of health spending and access to health care.

Seeking to reconcile these contrasting perspectives, a third group of analysts has suggested that much depends on whether health rights litigation is individually or collectively focused: while individually focused litigation yields benefits only for individuals, collectively focused litigation has the potential to yield benefits for a large number of citizens.

This study examines Indonesia's experience with health rights litigation and assesses its implications for efforts to promote the right to health in developing countries in general. Such litigation was unheard of under Suharto's authoritarian New Order regime but it has become a feature of the country's health and political landscapes since the country transitioned to democracy in the late 1990s. The fall of the New Order triggered a process of constitutional and legislative change that saw, among many other revisions to Indonesian law, the introduction of new provisions to the 1945 constitution and the enactment of numerous pieces of new legislation that strengthened protection of the right to health. Along with broader political and judicial reforms, this encouraged Indonesian citizens to take demands for health-related entitlements to court, leading to a series of court cases in which the right to health was explicitly invoked in legal argument and testimony.

This study argues that this litigation has served to promote fulfilment of the right to health in Indonesia by precipitating policy changes that helped to enforce it. This development has been supported by—and conditional upon—a number of factors, including a) the presence of judicial and health institutions that have limited the scope for citizens to engage in individually focused litigation and—instead—enabled them to engage in collectively oriented litigation; b) enhanced responsiveness by the political elite (including the judiciary) to social policy concerns as a result of the combined effects of the Asian economic crisis and democratization; and c) the presence of non-governmental organizations that have had a strong commitment to health rights, the financial and technical resources to mobilize the law, and the ability to forge alliances with and mobilize popular forces.

Litigation has served to promote fulfilment of the right to health in Indonesia by precipitating policy changes that helped to enforce it

As such, this study offers support to the third group of commentators above but, at the same time, points to a broader range of preconditions for rights-friendly change that go beyond the question of whether litigation is focused on individual or collective matters. Specifically, it contends that collectively oriented health rights litigation is only likely to have progressive effects when there is some degree of elite responsiveness to social policy concerns; the actors, resources, and alliances required to enable legal mobilization exist; and legal mobilization occurs in the context of wider political mobilization supportive of its aims. The last, the study suggests, is particularly important in this respect.

To support this argument, this study examines four cases of litigation in which the right to health was explicitly invoked either in legal argument or court testimony. These cases relate to: first, the Nunukan migrant workers tragedy (2002–2003); second, the corporatization of three local public hospitals in Jakarta (2004–2006); third, the enactment of legislation on social security providers (2009–2012); and fourth, the size of the central government's health budget (2010–2012). In the first three of these cases, it is argued, legal mobilization combined with various forms of political activism (such as demonstrations and media campaigns) led to judicial decisions that precipitated rights-friendly policy change. In the final case, legal mobilization failed to produce such change, at least directly and immediately, in part, because it was not accompanied by such political mobilization.

In terms of the broader implications of the analysis for efforts to promote fulfilment of the right to health in developing countries, the study makes three suggestions. The first is that changes to the institutional design of judicial and legal systems are necessary in countries that have experienced a high level of individually focused litigation. In particular, these countries should consider providing legal aid to the poor so that they have the same opportunity as middle-class citizens to lodge individual health rights claims; and they should institute mechanisms requiring judges to balance concerns with the fulfilment of individuals' health rights against an awareness of their redistributive and macro-economic impact. Second, health rights litigation is most likely to be effective where the broader political and social environment supports the fulfilment of health rights. Accordingly, proponents of the right to health should look for ways to maximize the conduciveness of this environment. This could be done, for instance, by providing financial support to non-governmental organizations to ensure that they have the financial and technical resources to engage in legal mobilization. Third, health rights litigation is most effective when supported by political mobilization. As such, legal and political mobilization should not be seen as separate, mutually exclusive options but components of a unified strategy for promoting health rights.

Litigating the Right to Health
Courts, Politics, and Justice in Indonesia

Introduction

Since the early 2000s, courts have become important players in struggles over the right to health in Indonesia as they have in many other developing countries in recent years.[1] Following the fall of Suharto's New Order regime in 1998, successive Indonesian governments have introduced legislative changes that have strengthened legal protections of this right. Health rights were also included in amendments to Indonesia's 1945 constitution.

These actions have encouraged Indonesian citizens to present their demands for health-related entitlements in terms of legally enforceable claims and, in some cases, attempt to realize these demands through the court system. This study examines this trend towards the "judicialization" of the right to health (Biehl et al. 2009; Yamin 2014, 1) in Indonesia. It asks: What has been the impact of health rights litigation in Indonesia? Has this litigation primarily served middle-class or corporate interests because they have had easier access to the courts? Or has it helped subaltern groups such as workers, peasants, or members of local communities? If so, under what conditions? Finally, it asks: What are the implications of Indonesia's experience with health rights litigation for efforts to promote fulfilment of the right to health in developing countries in general?

Proponents of rights-based approaches to health have argued that health rights litigation can have transformative effects, potentially triggering change with "a huge impact nationally, and even globally" (International Development Law Organization 2010, 2; see also Khan and Petrasek 2014). To support this view they have pointed to cases such as the Treatment Action Campaign in South Africa and public interest litigation in India, both of which have yielded important judicial and policy decisions improving ordinary citizens' access to health care and/or medication.[2] However other authors have been skeptical of the effectiveness of the litigation approach. They point to, among others, recent analyses of health rights litigation in several Latin American countries which have found that such litigation has often had regressive effects, particularly when it has taken the form of individualized claims for access to expensive medication or health services at public expense (Ferraz 2009; 2011; Bergallo 2011; Young and Lemaitre 2013; Flood and Gross 2014). This is because middle-class individuals—sometimes with the backing of pharmaceutical companies—have been better able than the poor, given the costs involved, to engage in such litigation.

Besides the proponents and skeptics of health litigation, a third group has taken a more nuanced approach. In a review of several countries' experiences with social rights litigation (a category including litigation related to education rights as well as to health rights), Brinks and Gauri (2014) distinguished between individually focused litigation and litigation concerned with the interests of broad groups (such as, for instance, litigation that addresses policy issues). Individually focused litigation, they showed, has generally only yielded benefits for the individuals who have been wealthy enough to fund it. By contrast, collectively focused litigation carried out by activists at non-governmental organizations (NGOs) and politically engaged citizens has often brought benefits for large groups of people, including—and particularly—the poor and marginalized. Collective legal action has, in practice, made a more substantial contribution to fulfilment of the right to health.

This study argues that health rights litigation in Indonesia has had broadly progressive effects, helping poor and marginalized citizens enhance or protect their right to health in practice by precipitating policy changes consistent with this outcome. In part this has been because institutional features of the country's judicial and health systems have limited the scope for citizens to engage in individually focused health rights litigation while facilitating their ability to engage in collectively focused (especially policy-oriented) litigation. But this success has also been achieved because the country's political elite (including its judiciary) has been relatively responsive to social policy concerns, due to the social impact of the 1997–1998 Asian economic crisis and the incentives created by democratization; and because the country has had NGOs that have a) espoused a strong commitment to the right to health; b) commanded the financial and technical resources to mobilize the law; and c) had the ability to forge alliances with subaltern groups, enabling large-scale political mobilization in support of efforts to promote change through the courts.

Consequently, this study points to a broader range of preconditions for socially inclusive outcomes in health rights litigation than simply the issue of whether this litigation is focused on individual or collective matters. Primarily the discussion suggests that the nature of this litigation—that is, whether it is individually or collectively focused—is itself a function of a country's judicial and health institutions.

Furthermore, this study proposes that collectively focused litigation is only likely to have progressive effects when there is some degree of elite (especially judicial) responsiveness to social policy demands; the actors, resources, and alliances required to enable legal mobilization are in place; and legal activism occurs in the context of wider political mobilization supportive of its aims.

None of these factors can be taken for granted. In terms of the broader implications for efforts to promote fulfilment of the right to health in developing countries, this study thus submits that attention needs to be given not just to the institutional design of judicial and health systems but also to measures that enhance the capacity of NGOs (or similar actors) to engage in legal and political mobilization and to do both simultaneously.

In presenting this analysis, this study begins by examining the position of the right to health in Indonesian law. Following sections explore how the nature and scope of health rights litigation have been shaped by the country's judicial and health institutions; the degree of elite responsiveness to social policy concerns; and the presence of NGOs with the requisite financial resources, capacities, and alliances.

Points raised in these sections are subsequently illustrated by four case studies of health litigation. These cases relate to: first, the Nunukan migrant workers tragedy (2002–2003); second, the corporatization of three local public hospitals in Jakarta (2004–2006); third, the enactment of legislation on social security providers (*badan penyelenggara jaminan sosial*, BPJS; 2009–2012); and fourth, the size of the central government's health budget (2010–2012). The final section assesses the implications of the analysis for efforts to promote fulfilment of the right to health in developing countries in general.

Before beginning this analysis, it is necessary to briefly define the terms "right to health" and "health rights litigation" as they are used in this study.

The United Nations Committee on Economic, Social and Cultural Rights is the body responsible for monitoring implementation of the International Covenant on Economic, Social and Cultural Rights (the principal foundation of the right to health in international law). In *General Comment 14: The Right to the Highest Attainable Standard of Health* (United Nations Committee on Economic, Social and Cultural Rights 2000) it has interpreted the right to health in expansive terms. Specifically, the committee has stated that the right to health entails "a right to the enjoyment of a variety of facilities, goods, services, and conditions necessary for the realization of the highest attainable standard of health" (Article 9).

> *The right to health incorporates not merely a right to health care but also a right to the underlying preconditions for health*

According to this definition, the right to health incorporates not merely a right to health care but also a right to the underlying preconditions for health such as access to water, food, and sanitation; the fulfilment of basic needs; and the presence of a healthy environment.

This study adopts the committee's definition. Going even further, however, the study acknowledges that there is a close connection between the right to health and other rights (e.g., the right to social security, specifically as this relates to access to health care) and associated state obligations (e.g., to provide health services). Accordingly, this study defines health rights litigation as cases that a) make claims based on constitutional, legislative, or internationally recognized rights to health, related rights, or associated state obligations; b) seek access to health facilities, goods, and services; or c) concern the underlying preconditions for health.[3] Importantly for the purposes of the study, this definition excludes litigation involving civil or criminal claims against health professionals or health service providers (as is the case, for instance, in malpractice suits; Gloppen and Roseman 2011, 15).

The Right to Health in Indonesian Law

The right to health is a relatively recent addition to Indonesian law. During the New Order, Indonesian law provided little protection for this right. The original version of the 1945 constitution, which was in force in unrevised form under the New Order, stated that each citizen had a right to a "way of living that is appropriate for humanity" (Article 27 (2)). Other than this, however, it did not provide protection for any other dimension of the right to health. Law 23/1992 on health, the New Order's main piece of health-related legislation, stated that "everyone has the same right to obtain an optimal standard of health" (Article 4) but did not explicitly provide Indonesian citizens with a right to health care or the preconditions for health. In Article 7, it stated that the government "has the role ('*bertugas*') of carrying out health efforts that are equitable and accessible by the people." At most, this only *implied* that citizens have a right to health.

Following the fall of the New Order, the Majelis Permusyawaratan Rakyat (MPR, People's Consultative Assembly), the highest legislative body in the country, amended the 1945 constitution. The amendments, which were carried out between 1999 and 2002, included the addition of a bill of rights based on the Universal Declaration of Human Rights (UDHR). This particular amendment (Chapter XA), adopted in 2000, was designed as a response to widespread criticism about the New Order's human rights record (Lindsey 2008, 29).

Among other changes, the adding of the human rights clauses saw the introduction of new rights "to obtain health services" (Article 28H (1)), to "have a good and healthy living environment" (Article 28H

(1)), to have access to social security (Article 28H (3)), and to "develop oneself through the fulfilment of basic needs" (Article 28C (1)). In accordance with these new rights, the MPR also incorporated into the constitution a new obligation for the state to provide "health service facilities" (Article 34 (3)) and declared that the state would develop a social security system for all people (Article 34 (2)). Amid and in the wake of these amendments, the national parliament (Dewan Perwakilan Rakyat, DPR) enacted a number of laws that reaffirmed—and in some cases expanded upon—the abovementioned constitutional rights and obligations. These new laws included:

- *Law 39/1999 on Human Rights*, which provided all people with rights to a healthy environment, fulfilment of basic needs, and social security. It also provided children with a right to health services.
- *Law 23/2002 on Child Protection*, which reaffirmed children's right to health services and provided them with a right to social security. It also imposed an obligation on the state to provide "comprehensive" health services and programs to ensure "optimal" levels of health for all children.
- *Law 29/2004 on Medical Practice,* which established an obligation for doctors to provide medical services in accordance with professional standards, operational procedures, and patients' medical needs. It did not, however, require that these services be provided for free, noting that doctors had a right to receive payment for their services.
- *Law 32/2004 on Regional Government,* which created an obligation for regional governments to provide health-service facilities and develop a social security system in carrying out regional autonomy.
- *Law 40/2004 on a National Social Security System,* which established specific rights for citizens and obligations for state agencies with regards to social security.
- *Law 11/2005 on the Ratification of the International Covenant on Economic, Social and Cultural Rights,* which endorsed all rights provided for in this covenant, including the right to the highest attainable standard of health.
- *Law 36/2009 on Health*, which provided citizens with rights to health, a healthy environment, and health services that are safe, meet a minimum level of quality, and are accessible. It also im-

posed various corresponding obligations on the state—such as to deliver health services, provide health information and education, and protect the environment.

- *Law 44/2009 on Hospitals,* which detailed various rights and responsibilities for both hospitals and patients.
- *Law 36/2014 on Medical Workers,* which noted that "health as a human right has to be fulfilled in the form of provision of various health services to all citizens" (Article b, Preamble). It also imposed an obligation on health workers to provide health services in accordance with various professional, operational, and ethical standards as well as patients' needs. However, as with doctors under Law 29/2004, Law 36/2014 gave health workers permission to receive payment in exchange for their services.
- *Law 38/2014 on Nursing,* which provided "clients" with a right to obtain nursing services in accordance with various professional, operational, and ethical standards. It also imposed an obligation on nurses to provide such services in accordance with these standards. Similar to Laws 29/2004 and 36/2014, it allowed for charging of fees for services rendered.

Indonesian Health Rights Litigation: The Role of Judicial and Health Institutions

There are considerable practical difficulties in identifying court cases related to specific subjects in Indonesia. Information and data on decisions made by Indonesian courts are limited (Susanti 2008, 230). However, in broad terms, health rights litigation in Indonesia appears to have been collectively focused. This stands in contrast to the practice in many Latin American countries, where such litigation has been concentrated on claims by individuals for access to health services or medication to address their particular needs. In particular, health rights litigation in Indonesia has often had a central concern with health-policy issues. There are four primary reasons for the collective focus of Indonesian health rights litigation, all of which relate to the institutional design of Indonesia's judicial and health systems.

First, Indonesia's judicial system does not include a mechanism for individual claims related to breaches of constitutional rights of the sort that have characterized the Latin American experience. Under current law, Indonesians can file judicial reviews to challenge the constitutionality of a statute, but they cannot file a constitutional complaint against a specific government action they view as unconstitutional. This is starkly different from the *amparo*-style[4] court actions against individual breaches of constitutional rights common to many Latin American countries. There, such actions have been the principal pathway through which citizens have brought cases against the state to secure access to expensive medicine or health services—mostly on the grounds that denial of such access is a breach of their constitutional right to health (Young and Lemaitre 2013).

Like their Latin American counterparts, many Indonesian citizens have experienced difficulty in accessing medicines and health services through the public health system. Legal and illegal fees for health services and medicines have discouraged many poor people from using public health services, while the low quality of such services has encouraged many middle-class Indonesians to use private clinics and hospitals. At the same time, doctor absenteeism and the absence of medicine supplies are commonplace at public health facilities, as is deliberate prescription of inappropriate medicines and referral to doctors' or nurses' private practices (Buehler 2008; World Bank 2009b; Rosser 2012; National Team for the Acceleration of Poverty Reduction 2015, 2). But in the absence of *amparo*-style mechanisms, there has been no easily available legal avenue for Indonesian citizens—whether poor or middle class—to try to address this situation by filing individualized claims against constitutional breaches centered on the right to health.[5] This, in turn, has pushed litigants to pursue collective action.

Many Indonesian citizens have experienced difficulty in accessing medicines and health services through the public health system

Second, Indonesia lacked—at least until 2014—a universal, mandatory, and national public health insurance scheme akin to those in some Latin American countries. Such schemes contributed to the massive increase in individually focused health rights litigation in Latin America by giving all citizens (including, most importantly, middle-class citizens) an entitlement to certain specified services and medicine.

This fuelled a sense of entitlement to free health care and medication more generally. Most health rights litigation in these countries has related either to medicine or services that are covered under these schemes or for which there is no clear rationale for their exclusion (Wilson 2011; Young and Lemaitre 2013, 187–88; Flood and Gross 2014, 67–68; Thompson 2015, 2).

In Indonesia, on the other hand, the poor and near poor have been covered by a succession of rather fragmented government-funded health insurance programs introduced in the post–New Order period: first, Asuransi Kesehatan Masyarakat Miskin (ASKESKIN, health insurance for the poor; 2004–2008), and subsequently, Jaminan Kesehatan Masyarakat (JAMKESMAS, community health insurance; 2008–2014), which targeted the poor and near poor. In 2014, a mandatory national health insurance scheme (Jaminan Kesehatan Nasional, JKN) was established, which will provide universal coverage when fully rolled out.[6] The government pays the JKN premiums for the poor and near poor—in 2015, a total of 86 million people.

Prior to 2014, civil servants, retired military officials, and private-sector workers were covered by government-run schemes specifically focused on them—Asuransi Kesehatan untuk Pegawai Negeri Sipil dan Pensiunan TNI/POLRI (ASKES, health insurance for civil servants and retired armed forces personnel) in the case of civil servants and retired military officials, and Jaminan Sosial Tenaga Kerja (JAMSOSTEK, social insurance for private-sector workers) in the case of private-sector workers. Since 2014, JKN has covered these three sets of workers as well, but they are expected to pay their own premiums based on the quality of the insurance coverage they choose.

Many middle-class Indonesians have, however, continued to rely on private health insurance, either because they were initially excluded from government-run schemes (as, for instance, in the cases of ASKESKIN and JAMKESMAS) or they avoided joining schemes they found unattractive (as in the case of JAMSOSTEK).[7] At the time of writing, it appears that many middle-class Indonesians have also failed to join JKN despite its mandatory nature, mostly because of reluctance by private businesses to sign on to the scheme.[8] This disjointed development of public health care schemes has constrained the emergence of a sense of entitlement to health services and medication at public expense among citizens and thus reduced the potential of specific claimants choosing the path of individualized rights-based litigation. Instead, Indonesian citizens interested in claiming health rights have primarily opted to challenge health policy as such through collective action.

Third, while there has been no easily accessible judicial mechanism for individual claims against the state for breaches of constitutional rights, there is an avenue for collective claims against the state for rights breaches, namely class action suits. Class action suits are a complex form of litigation. To be successful, they must have a clear legal basis (which can include a breach of the right to health), specify and justify the damages sought, and demonstrate that each plaintiff has suffered a loss as a result of the relevant action or inaction. Nevertheless, they have become increasingly common in Indonesia—according to Santosa (2007), for instance, there were 20–30 class action suits in Indonesia in the decade between 1997, when this form of litigation was first recognized in Indonesian law, and 2007—even if many have proven unsuccessful. Some class action suits have related to the right to health, particularly issues such as environmental pollution, fake medicines, and unsafe food (see, for instance, Susanti 2008). In late 2016, for instance, the Yayasan Lembaga Konsumen Indonesia (YLKI, Indonesian Consumers Foundation) was preparing a class action against the use of fake health vaccines in several hospitals over a period of 13 years. In this case, the class action was aimed at exposing and challenging the government's failure as a health regulator and oversight body.

Fourth and finally, the fall of the New Order opened up a range of new opportunities for citizens to launch policy-related litigation and to do so in particular by invoking rights and/or associated state obligations provided for in the 1945 constitution and laws. This occurred not just because of the sort of legislative and constitutional changes discussed above but also because the broader process of democratization entailed judicial reforms that expanded the role of Indonesian courts in policy-making and enhanced the accessibility to the court system for ordinary citizens and NGOs. These changes have been discussed elsewhere in detail (Crouch 2010, 191–241; Tahyar 2012; Rosser 2015b; Butt and Parsons 2014).

The post-1998 reforms to the political and legal macro-framework yielded a situation in which citizens and NGOs could use at least three legal avenues to influence government health policy by invoking the right to health.

To begin with, there is the option of *judicial review of laws by the Constitutional Court*. Under the New Order, the judiciary had no authority to rule on the constitutionality of laws passed by the national parliament and its individual articles. Following the fall of the New Order, the Constitutional Court, established in 2003, was given this authority (along with certain other powers).[9] While lawmakers did not allow the Constitutional Court to hear complaints about the breach of individual constitutional rights, the court itself devised administrative and legal standing rules that allowed citizens and NGOs relatively easy access to court to challenge statutes.

For instance, the Constitutional Court decided to charge no administrative costs, reducing the financial barriers to lodging a judicial review request at the court (Asshiddiqie 2006, 135). It also granted legal standing to NGOs, enabling them (as well as individual citizens) to submit judicial review requests to the court (Hendrianto 2016, 25). Along with other changes discussed here, the result was to make the Constitutional Court an

> *Given the rights in the amended 1945 constitution, many constitutional challenges to laws were filed based on rights-based grounds*

important site for contesting government policy. Given the rights provided for in the amended 1945 constitution, many of the constitutional challenges to laws were filed based on rights-based grounds.

The second avenue is *judicial review of regulations by the Supreme Court*. Under the New Order, the Supreme Court had authority to review regulations and decrees for consistency with laws. But this authority was severely circumscribed. For instance, the Supreme Court had no authority to strike down regulations and decrees—it could only declare them in breach of the law. Further, it could only hear requests for judicial review on appeal from lower courts. The fall of the New Order saw the court's powers of judicial review strengthened, allowing for direct challenges to regulations/decrees (rather than merely via appeal), and enabling it to strike down regulations and decrees (Butt and Parsons 2014, 70–71). While it has charged administrative fees—making it a more expensive option than the Constitutional Court for actors seeking to challenge government policy through judicial review—these costs have not been prohibitive.[10] Its rules addressing legal standing have also been liberal, allowing NGOs as well as citizens to lodge requests for judicial review. As a result, the Supreme Court has also become a key site for contesting government policy—and with constitutionally provided rights often filtering down into lower-level laws and regulations relevant to Supreme Court judgments, many cases have been pursued on rights-based grounds as well.

Lastly, there are also *citizen lawsuits*. Citizen lawsuits are a type of civil action allowing citizens to challenge government action or inaction that breaches the law and causes harm to members of the public or the public interest. They are similar to class actions but are simpler to put together and harder to challenge because they do not entail requests for damages. Nor do citizen lawsuits require plaintiffs to demonstrate that they have each suffered a loss as a result of the relevant government action/inaction (Hermawanto 2009, 500–503). As such, they are typically aimed at changing government policy, improving the implementation of policy, or forcing the government to introduce/implement policy where it has not yet done so.

Citizen lawsuits were unknown in Indonesia's legal system until 2003, when the Central Jakarta District Court accepted them as a legitimate form of civil action in the Nunukan migrant workers case (one of the cases examined below; Susanti 2008, 252). Since then, they have been used in several cases, including those related to the national exam (Rosser 2015b) and the 2004 and 2011 social security laws (another of the cases discussed below).

The collectively focused nature of health rights litigation in Indonesia, shaped by the factors described above, has been relatively conducive to rights-friendly outcomes compared to individually focused litigation. But this has not meant that such outcomes have been inevitable. The following sections show that the impact of health rights litigation in Indonesia has also been facilitated by the degree of elite (including judicial) responsiveness to social policy concerns, as well as by the nature, capacities, and alliances of NGOs. In combination, these sections suggest that NGOs' capacity for alliance building and political mobilization to accompany efforts to promote change through the courts has been particularly important in shaping outcomes.

Indonesian Health Rights Litigation: Supported by Elite Responsiveness to Social Policy Concerns

The responsiveness of post-1998 elites—including in the judiciary— to social policy pressures has been a decisive factor in encouraging collective health rights litigation. During the New Order period, the political elite gave a relatively low priority to social policy. To the extent that the government invested significant resources in social policy, it prioritized a) the needs of military and bureaucratic officials and, to a much lesser extent, formal private-sector workers and b) investments that served to promote economic growth, in particular by ensuring political and social stability.

For instance, the government established no pension and health insurance schemes for the unemployed or informal private-sector workers.[11] By contrast, it generously subsidized pension and health insurance schemes for military and bureaucratic officials: ASKES, which, as noted earlier, provided health insurance for civil servants and retired military officials; Tabungan dan Asuransi Pegawai Negeri (TASPEN), which provided pensions for civil servants; and Asuransi Sosial Angkatan Bersenjata Republik Indonesia (ASABRI, social insurance for armed forces personnel), which provided pensions for military officials. The government also ran a pension and health insurance scheme for formal private-sector workers, namely JAMSOSTEK, although, as noted earlier, this offered limited benefits and was widely evaded (Ramesh 2014, 43). Finally, the government subsidized the price of rice, the country's dominant staple food. The subsidy was intended, primarily, to promote political and social stability by reducing the potential for food shortages, something that had contributed to the instability of the preceding Guided Democracy regime.

In this respect, Indonesia adhered broadly to the "productivist" model of welfare capitalism widely considered characteristic of the East Asian region as a whole (Rosser and van Diermen 2016). The defining features of this "productivist" model are the subordination of social policy to economic policy and the presence of a growth-oriented state (Holliday 2000). Countries following this model typically invest little in social programs and, to the extent that they do, prioritize provision of welfare to "productive" elements in society (e.g., formal private-sector workers, civil servants, and military officials) and areas that promote economic growth.

The Asian economic crisis and ensuing demise of the New Order regime, however, changed Indonesia's situation in this respect. The crisis plunged millions into poverty and raised fears that health service utilization and school enrolments would fall sharply (see, for instance, Stalker 2000, 5–8). For all their notorious self-indulgence, Indonesia's political elites appear to have been shocked by the crisis' impact on the country's social fabric, forcing them to rethink their approach to welfare policies.

At the same time, democratization created an incentive for these elites to promote social policies favoring the poor and marginalized, given the electoral appeal of such policies. It also removed obstacles to groups that had previously been excluded from the policy-making process, such as NGOs and citizens groups with an interest in social policy issues. Further, democratization opened up new policy spaces, including regular public consultations by the national parliament as part of legislative processes, a freer media, and the new legal pathways discussed earlier (Rosser, Roesad, and Edwin 2005) that these actors could access to influence policy.

Within this context, the government's approach to social policy became more progressive in nature. Under the influence of technocratic officials and their allies in the donor community, the government introduced a range of policy reforms aimed at promoting the decentralization of public education and health services; the corporatization of public health and education service providers; greater competition in the provision of health and education services; and improved service quality through the introduction of new accreditation arrangements (Rosser 2016; Sujudi et al. 2004).

It tempered this shift with a range of social protection schemes designed to protect the poor and vulnerable

At the same time, however, it tempered this shift towards a more market-oriented approach with a range of social protection schemes designed to, for the most part, protect the poor and vulnerable. During the crisis, the government introduced "social safety net" schemes supported with funds from the World Bank and the Asian Development

Bank (ADB) to help the poor maintain their living standards. Generally referred to as the "first generation" of social protection programs, these ran until the early 2000s.

At this time the government began to introduce a "second generation" of programs funded largely through cuts to government fuel subsidies that had mostly benefitted the middle class and businesses. These included redesigned versions of several "first generation" schemes plus new conditional and unconditional cash-transfer schemes (Sumarto and Bazzi 2011). The most substantial of these programs were Bantuan Operasional Sekolah (BOS, school operational assistance), a school grants scheme aimed at providing free basic education; Bantuan Langsung Tunai (BLT, temporary direct cash assistance), an unconditional cash transfer scheme targeting the poor; Beras Untuk Keluarga Miskin (RASKIN, rice subsidy for poor families), a program aimed at providing rice to the poor; ASKESKIN and JAMKESMAS, health insurance programs which, as noted earlier, provided free health care to the poor and near poor respectively; and the Program Nasional Pemberdayaan Masyarakat (PNPM, community empowerment program), a scheme that funds village-level development projects.

For the purposes of this study, two developments were especially important. The first was the appointment of Siti Fadillah Supari as minister of health in 2004 following Susilo Bambang Yudhoyono's election as president that year. A relative political unknown prior to her appointment, Supari, in keeping with the radical populist tradition in Indonesian economic thinking,[12] emerged as a strong critic of neoliberal health policies (Bari 2009; Supari 2010). She voiced stinging criticisms of the World Health Organization (WHO) and the World Bank and of Anglo-American donors who supported their policies, and she dramatically reduced Ministry of Health cooperation with these organizations.[13]

Partners for Health Alliance, a grouping that brought together foreign donors and the government around health issues, fell apart during her tenure as minister.[14] At one point she accused the WHO and the United States of a conspiracy relating to the use of Indonesian bird flu virus strains. Claiming that the WHO had shared these strains with laboratories in the United States that made vaccines, she asserted that the United States then sold these vaccines back to Indonesia and other developing countries at inflated prices (Thompson 2008).

Consistent with her radical populist orientation, Supari championed initiatives such as ASKESKIN and JAMKESMAS, apparently seeing them as a way to redistribute resources to the poor. This championing, in turn, built a political base for Supari within the public health system, gained her popularity, and better positioned her for either reappointment to the cabinet at the end of Yudhoyono's first term in 2009 or possible promotion to the vice presidency (she ultimately failed to realize either of these ambitions; Rosser 2012, 265). She also, as will be addressed below, played a key role in defeating moves to corporatize public hospitals.

The second important development was growing judicial activism in the area of human rights, including social rights. Under the New Order, judges were widely regarded as "gormless and corrupt functionaries who do the government's bidding in the government's courts" (Bourchier 1999, 233). To some extent, they have remained so in the post–New Order period (Tahyar 2012). But the judicial reforms mentioned above have nevertheless widened the scope for greater judicial activism in relation to human rights issues.[15] On the one hand, as noted above, these reforms created new legal pathways through which citizens and NGOs concerned about breaches of human rights could access the judicial system, especially for the purposes of collective litigation. On the other hand, these reforms also gave the judiciary greater independence from the executive, making it easier for judges to hand down decisions contrary to government positions considered to breach human rights. The reforms also created an opportunity for judges to build a political base among the poor and marginalized, both as a way of securing legitimacy for their respective courts and, in the case of some judges, positioning themselves for higher-level political office.

The Constitutional Court, in particular, became a locus for such activism, especially under its first two chief justices, Jimly Asshiddiqie and Mahfud MD. Its judicial selection and funding arrangements gave it a greater degree of autonomy from government than other Indonesian courts (Mietzner 2010), while the country's new rights-rich constitution provided the court with strong legal grounds for rights-friendly decisions.

Asshiddiqie and Mahfud both adopted the mantle of reformers while serving as chief justices (Hendrianto 2016). Mahfud, for his part, pursued an approach he termed "progressive law" (Budiarti 2013, 1–14), presumably in an effort to build popularity among the poor and marginalized for a subsequent tilt at the presidency or vice presidency (which he indeed sought in 2014, one year after his term ended).

However, the shift in favor of greater judicial activism appeared to permeate the court system as a whole. Even the Supreme Court, an institution widely seen as the most corrupt and dysfunctional element of the country's judicial system during the New Order (Pompe 2005), appeared to change direction. According to Butt and Parsons (2014, 71), the Supreme Court "appears no longer to feel constrained by the government in the exercise of its judicial powers…[It] has been willing to strike down laws issued by the government and even the president, something it would not have done during Soeharto's reign."

In relation to social policy, the result has been a set of judicial decisions that have challenged government efforts to promote neo-liberal reform in the social sectors and promote public health. These have included the Constitutional Court's decision on "education legal entities" (which annulled a law transforming public schools and universities into corporate bodies), its decision on "international standard schools" (which annulled legal provisions and regulations enabling the most popular public schools to charge fees and secure privileged access to state funding), its decisions on a series of central government budget laws (which pressured the central government to allocate 20 percent of budget spending to education as required under the amended constitution), and its decision on pictorial warnings on cigarettes (which made such warnings compulsory). Other significant court decisions included the Central Jakarta District Court's, the Jakarta High Court's, and the Supreme Court's respective decisions on the national school exam (which compelled the government to revise its policies so that exam results did not prevent students from continuing their education; Rosser and Curnow 2014; Rosser 2015a; 2015b).

Indonesian Health Rights Litigation: The Importance of NGO Activism

The impact of health rights litigation in Indonesia has also been shaped by the nature of the country's civil society and, in particular, its NGO community. During the New Order, the government pursued a strategy of disorganizing civil society through harsh restrictions on freedom of organization and expression, the establishment of state-sponsored corporatist organizations to control representation of key professional and social groups, and the co-optation or repression of organizations that existed outside these corporatist structures (Robison and Hadiz 2004, 120–44). In this context, the country's NGO community, although it grew strongly during the 1980s and 1990s, had enormous difficulty advocating effectively for the protection of human rights. At the same time, to the extent that it did engage in human rights advocacy, it tended to focus on issues of civil, political, land, environmental, and labor rights rather than the right to health.

This reflected the circumstance that the NGO community was one of the few sources of domestic opposition to the New Order and that the regime's authoritarianism and development strategy made it more vulnerable to criticisms of its breaches of the former set of rights than violations of

> *Health rights litigation in Indonesia has been shaped by the nature of the country's civil society and its NGO community*

the right to health. Further, while labor exploitation, forced removal of poor people from their land, and environmental degradation were domestic and international stains on the regime's reputation, it did achieve some successes in improving citizens' access to education and health services. As a result, NGO activism in this area was much lower profile.

The post–New Order period, however, witnessed the emergence of a collection of NGOs that became active in promoting the right to health in Indonesia. The fall of the New Order triggered the establishment of a small number of NGOs explicitly focused on social rights in general and the right to health in particular. Post-1998 Indonesia also saw many NGOs with a core focus on other issues become more engaged with the right to health as social policy became increasingly salient. This salience was mostly the result of activism by the above-mentioned new social/health-rights NGOs, as well as the new government initiatives to promote better social protection discussed in the previous section. Table 1 provides a list of some of the most prominent

Table 1. NGOs Engaged in Activism Related to the Right to Health in the Post–New Order Period

Name	Agenda and Activities
Yayasan Lembaga Bantuan Hukum Indonesia (YLBHI, Indonesian Legal Aid Foundation)	YLBHI was established in 1970 to provide legal aid to the poor. But, from the beginning, the organization focused on a broader agenda that included the development of a state based on the rule of law (*negara hukum*) and—subsequently—democratization. YLBHI had a particular interest in issues related to civil, political, land, labor, and environmental rights (Aspinall 2005, 100, 105). Following the fall of the New Order, YLBHI became involved in a number of political struggles and lawsuits related to the protection of social rights, with a special focus on education, and, to a lesser extent, health (Rosser 2015b).
Yayasan Lembaga Konsumen Indonesia (YLKI, Indonesian consumers foundation)	YLKI was established in the early 1970s to encourage Indonesian consumers to buy Indonesian products. Over time it transformed into a consumer rights organization. It also changed from being an elite-dominated NGO into one that is more critical of and oppositional in approach towards the government.[16] The work of YLKI has spanned a wide range of consumer rights issues. In the health sector, it has had particular concerns with tobacco control (Rosser 2015a) and hospital privatization.
Lembaga Bantuan Hukum Kesehatan (LBH Kesehatan, Health Legal Aid Institute)	LBH Kesehatan was established in 1996 to promote citizens' health rights as provided for in the 1992 Health Law (LBH Kesehatan n.d.). Currently led by lawyer Iskandar Sitorus, LBH Kesehatan operates simultaneously as an advocacy-oriented NGO and a commercial law firm.[17] It has been involved in activism (including litigation) related to medical malpractice, environmental health, and health insurance for the poor (Sirait 2004; Rosser 2012).
Indonesia Corruption Watch (ICW)	ICW was established in 1998, shortly after the fall of Suharto, and has become Indonesia's leading anti-corruption NGO. In the early 2000s it established a Public Services Monitoring Division to combat corruption in the education and health sectors.[18] In the health sector, ICW has been active in issues such as tobacco control and health insurance as well as in more general research and advocacy work on health-sector corruption (Rosser 2012; 2015a).
Yayasan Lembaga Pemberdayaan Konsumen Kesehatan Indonesia (YLPKKI, Indonesian Health Consumers Empowerment Foundation)	YLPKKI was established in 1998 to promote the rights of health consumers.[19] A small NGO without significant external support, it is currently led by Marius Widjajarta, formerly with the Indonesian Consumers Foundation (YLKI). Since establishing YLPKKI, Widjajarta has been active in issues such as medical malpractice, tobacco control, and the privatization of hospitals.[20] He is often quoted in the Indonesia media as an expert on health issues.

Name	Agenda and Activities
Forum Indonesia untuk Transparansi Anggaran (FITRA, Indonesian Forum for Budget Transparency)	FITRA was established in 1999 to promote good governance and social justice by improving budget transparency (FITRA n.d.). Together with Prakarsa, FITRA has supported the concept of a "constitutional budget"—one that embodies the explicit and implied commitments to education and health described in the 1945 constitution (Sucipto et al. 2015).
Koalisi untuk Indonesia Sehat (KuIS, Coalition for a Healthy Indonesia)	KuIS was established in 2000 to create a multi-stakeholder network of national and regional actors with presumed interests in improving Indonesia's health system and health outcomes. Led by Firman Lubis from the University of Indonesia's Public Health faculty, KuIS comprises professional medical associations, private companies, NGOs, and Islamic social organizations (such as Muhammadiyah and Nahdlatul Ulama). KuIS was initially supported with funding from the United States Agency for International Development and Johns Hopkins University. KuIS pushed for amendments to the 1992 health law, provided grants to regional affiliates, ran workshops and seminars on health issues, and produced a public health advocacy guide (Topatimasang et al. 2005; Witoelar 2000). KuIS is no longer active.
Institut Hak Ekosob (Institute for Ecosoc Rights)	The Institute for Ecosoc Rights was established in 2003 to carry out research on issues related to economic, social, and cultural rights and to provide support to NGOs and donors working on these issues.[21] The institute has been particularly active in supporting the rights of migrant workers but has also worked on indigenous, food, health, and education rights (Institute for Ecosoc Rights n.d.). It is currently led by Sri Palupi and has been supported with funding from a range of donor sources.
Prakarsa (Welfare Initiative for Better Societies)	Prakarsa was established in 2004 by activists associated with Indonesian NGO Forum on Indonesian Development (INFID) to promote social welfare policies and values by carrying out independent research and engaging with key stakeholders.[22] Prakarsa has advocated for the development of a welfare state (Triwibowo and Bahagijo 2006) and the concept of a "constitutional budget" (Sucipto et al. 2015). It has been supported financially by the Ford Foundation.[23]
Trade Union Rights Centre (TURC)	TURC was established in 2004 to support Indonesia's labor movement by carrying out research, training, and advocacy-related activities.[24] TURC has played a leading role in the political struggles concerning health insurance.
Serikat Rakyat Miskin Indonesia (SRMI, Indonesian Poor Peoples' League)	SRMI was established by radical left-wing activists in 2004 —initially as the Serikat Rakyat Miskin Kota (City Poor Peoples' League)—to fight for poor people's rights and promote their sovereignty. SRMI programs include working for people's rights to obtain free quality health services (Serikat Rakyat Miskin Indonesia n.d.).

Name	Agenda and Activities
Indonesian Human Rights Committee for Social Justice (IHCS)	IHCS was established in 2007 by former student activists, many of whom were lawyers. IHCS has focused on issues related to social rights, especially food, land, education, and health rights. It has often made strategic use of the court system. IHCS has been supported financially by Oxfam, an international NGO committed to rights-based approaches to development, and by Yayasan Tifa (the Tifa Foundation), the Indonesian arm of the Open Society.[25]
Dewan Kesehatan Rakyat (DKR, Peoples' Health Council)	DKR was established in 2008 to mobilize popular support for the government's health insurance program, JAMKESMAS. It has been closely aligned with Siti Fadilah Supari, Indonesia's health minister from 2004 to 2009.[26] DKR's activism is informed by radical political leanings, reflecting Supari's populist ideals (Bari 2009) and the fact that many of its activists were drawn from the Partai Rakyat Demokratik (PRD, Democratic People's Party), a left-wing party established in 1996.[27]

and important NGOs that have been involved in activism related to the right to health in the post–New Order period.

Importantly for this specific study, the NGOs commanded sufficient financial and legal resources between them to utilize the courts to promote the right to health. The development of these resources, in turn, was due to the NGOs' successes in tapping funding from external sources and the fact that many of them employed activist lawyers. Moreover, they increased their mobilization capacity by forging close links to other groups within civil society, including subaltern groups such as workers. As Hans Antlöv et al. (Antlöv, Ibrahim, and van Tuijl 2006, 74) noted, the leadership of traditional Indonesian NGOs had generally been university educated, aspired to middle-class status, and had little knowledge of grassroots mobilization. Consequently, there was—and, in some cases, continues to be—a "great distance between NGOs and the communities they were working for, geographically, culturally, socially and economically." By contrast, this particular set of NGOs has had some success in building alliances with other sections of civil society, enhancing their collective capacity to engage in legal and political mobilization to promote the right to health.

Two groups were particularly important partners for health rights NGOs.

The first was critically minded public health intellectuals. Enhanced academic freedom created greater space for academics and other intellectuals to engage in health-policy debates, with figures such as Hasbullah Thabrany and Ascobat Gani (both from the University of Indonesia's public health faculty) and Laksono Trisnantoro (from Gadjah Mada University's medical faculty) being especially vocal in this respect (see, for instance, Thabrany et al. 2003; Thabrany 2005; Trisnantoro 2003; 2010). Skeptical of neoliberal health-policy reforms and committed to the right to health, these figures made natural allies for the NGOs.

The second section of civil society that formed partnerships with health rights NGOs was the trade union movement. The elimination of restrictions on freedom of organization, expression, and ideological orientation led to the establishment of new trade unions which were independent of the New Order's corporatist bodies. Whereas the New Order only recognized one labor federation, by 2002 there were 62 national trade federations—often competing with each other—registered with the Manpower Ministry (Rosser, Roesad, and Edwin 2005, 62). As we will see, while the trade unions have been predominantly concerned with matters of industrial relations policy such as the minimum wage, they were persuaded to broaden their agenda to embrace the issue of social welfare in the late 2000s by a set of public health academics and NGO activists committed to the right to health.[28]

Litigating Health Rights: Four Cases

This section examines the effects of health rights litigation in Indonesia—and the factors that shaped it—by analyzing four cases of litigation. These relate to: a) the Nunukan migrant workers tragedy (2002–2003); b) the corporatization of three local public hospitals in Jakarta (2004–2006); c) the enactment of legislation on social security providers (BPJS) (2009–2012); and d) the size of the central government's health budget (2010–2012). All of these cases involved collective, rather than individual, claims and focused largely on policy issues, reflecting the influence of the institutional factors pertaining to the legal- and health-system designs discussed above. As indicated, they show that the impact of health rights litigation in Indonesia has been influenced not just by the collectively focused nature of this litigation but also by the degree of elite (including judicial) responsiveness to social policy concerns, as well as the nature, capacities, and alliances of NGOs. The cases are examined below in chronological order.

Case 1: The Nunukan Migrant Workers Tragedy

Since the New Order period, Indonesia has developed into a major exporter of labor, particularly to countries in the Middle East and in Asia. In 2015, Indonesia ranked 14th among the world's recipients of migrant remittances, with an estimated $10.5 billion sent from its workers living abroad, securing livelihoods for millions of Indonesians at home (Al Azhari and Bisara 2016).

The Indonesian government has actively encouraged this outward labor migration because of these economic benefits. Critics, however, have suggested that it has done little to ensure that migrant workers' rights are adequately protected while they are in transit or overseas between Indonesia and their destination. Indeed, Indonesian migrant workers are highly vulnerable while they are in transit or overseas. The vast majority are female and are employed as domestic workers in people's homes well away from the protective oversight of trade unions, NGOs, or the media. A smaller number, mostly male, are employed in formal private-sector occupations in the construction, plantation, and manufacturing industries. Many Indonesians travel overseas for work on fake documents. Reports of rape, physical abuse, intimidation, low pay, and poor working conditions for Indonesian migrant workers are common (Ford 2006, 315–16; International Organization for Migration 2010).

One of the main destinations of Indonesian migrant workers is Malaysia, leading to frequent tensions between the two nations. In May 2002, the Malaysian government passed new immigration legislation that imposed harsh sanctions on illegal workers, including caning, fines, and jail sentences. This forced around a half million Indonesian workers to return to their home country, especially in the weeks leading up to August 1, 2002, when the legislation was implemented (*Jakarta Post* 2002a; Nunukan Humanitarian Tragedy Advocacy Team 2003, 12–13).

The legislation had been issued to address growing job insecurity in Malaysia after the Asian economic crisis, media reports about crimes committed by Indonesian migrant workers, and growing concerns about terrorist activity in the wake of 9/11 (Liow 2003, 48–50). Following their departure from Malaysia, many of the returned workers were transported to Nunukan in East Kalimantan, where they became stranded without adequate access to food, water, shelter, sanitation, or health services. Many fell ill as a result of such infections as diarrhea, malaria, or dysentery, causing the deaths of more than 80 people. Health issues were thus at the center of the tragedy (Ministry of Health 2003, 15–19; Nunukan Humanitarian Tragedy Advocacy Team 2003, 18–19).

A group of Indonesian NGOs mobilized to assist the returned migrants by providing them with humanitarian aid and medical services as well as promoting awareness of their plight through the mass media. Calling themselves the Jaringan Relawan Kemanusiaan untuk Nunukan (JRKN, Volunteers' Humanitarian Network for Nunukan), this group included migrants', women's, and human rights NGOs. The Yayasan Lembaga Bantuan Hukum Indonesia (YLBHI, Indonesian Legal Aid Foundation) and the Jakarta Social Institute (the organization out of which the Institute for Ecosoc Rights grew, see Table 1) were at the forefront of the campaign (*Jakarta Post* 2002b).[29]

> *Indonesian NGOs mobilized to assist the returned migrants by providing them with humanitarian aid and medical services*

The government, by contrast, was slow to respond, doing little to assist the migrant workers until September 2002 (Ministry of Health 2003, 20–38). When it did, its assistance was insufficient for the scale of the tragedy, poorly organized, and undermined by corruption (Nunukan Humanitarian Tragedy Advocacy Team 2003, 21–22). Nevertheless, by early December 2002, the crisis had abated, with most of the migrant workers and their families returning to their homes in Indonesia or going back, now with the appropriate papers, to Malaysia for work (Kuswardono et al. 2002).

In January 2003, the JRKN lodged a citizen lawsuit at the Central Jakarta District Court—the first case of its kind—to demand that the government adopt new policies offering better protection for Indonesian migrant workers, including better access to adequate health services upon return from overseas. The group had decided to pursue this form of lawsuit—notwithstanding its uncertain foundations in Indonesian law—in part because of the inherent obstacles to pursuing individual claims against the state; in part because of the difficulties associated with class actions; and in part because a key objective was to change government policy, something that could potentially be done through a citizen lawsuit.[30]

The lawsuit listed 53 individuals as plaintiffs (*penggugat*), including a collection of NGO activists, public figures, former migrant workers, and student activists. The plaintiffs were supported by a team of lawyers from YLBHI, the Trade Union Rights Centre (TURC; see Table 1), and other NGOs and an array of experts and witnesses, all of whom provided their assistance and expertise pro bono. YLBHI covered the costs of the court case (Nunukan Humanitarian Tragedy Advocacy Team 2003; Pengadilan Negeri Jakarta Pusat 2003).[31]

In legal terms, the citizen lawsuit centered on Article 1365 of the Civil Code on unlawful acts (Susanti 2008, 251). The plaintiffs and their lawyers argued that the Indonesian government had committed an unlawful act by failing to protect the Nunukan migrant workers. They claimed that Indonesia's citizenry, as represented by the 53 plaintiffs, was therefore entitled to restitution in the form of various government actions. Specifically, the plaintiffs demanded that the Central Jakarta District Court instruct the government to, among other things, enact a new law on migrant workers that would provide such workers with better protection; ratify the *UN Convention on the Rights of All Migrant Workers and Members of their Families*; negotiate a bilateral agreement with Malaysia that would offer protection to migrant workers' rights and those of their families; and present a demand for compensation to the Malaysian government on behalf of the migrant workers who were stranded at Nunukan (Nunukan Humanitarian Tragedy Advocacy Team 2003, 25–26). Importantly for our purposes, in their legal arguments the plaintiffs and their lawyers pointed to the ways in which the government's negligence had breached migrant workers' constitutional right to obtain health services and the associated state obligation to provide health-service facilities (Nunukan Humanitarian Tragedy Advocacy Team 2003, 22–23).

In its decision, made in December 2003, the court accepted the citizen lawsuit as a legitimate form of civil action, found that the government had provided insufficient protection to Indonesian migrant workers, and sentenced the government to "take concrete steps" to improve their management of migrant workers and their families. The court also ordered the government to pay court costs (Pengadilan Negeri Jakarta Pusat 2003).

Otherwise, it dismissed the plaintiffs' case, refusing to state that the government had been negligent or instruct the government to change its laws and international commitments. But because its decision entailed rejection of key parts of the government's defense against the lawsuit and permitted a new form of litigation, this decision was widely seen as a "legal breakthrough" and an act of judicial activism (*Hukum Online* 2003). Sensing that this case could set a precedent for further similar lawsuits, the government decided to lodge an appeal to the Jakarta High Court. With the public campaign around the Nunukan tragedy having by that point faded into the past, the Jakarta High Court sided with the government. It found that the government had not committed an unlawful act and, hence, that the plaintiff's case should be dismissed in its entirety (*Hukum Online* 2006).

Despite this conclusion, the citizen lawsuit was moderately successful in terms of its broader objective: that is, to pressure the government to change its policies vis-à-vis the protection of migrant workers' rights. Importantly, this included the right to health services, especially upon return to Indonesia. In the year after the Nunukan trial, the Indonesian parliament passed Law 39/2004 on the Placement and Protection of Indonesian Migrant Workers. The new statute included articles on the protection of migrant workers' rights upon return to Indonesia and outlined the government's obligations in this respect. For instance, Article 7e imposed an obligation on the government to provide protection to Indonesian migrant workers before, during, and *after* their overseas placements and Article 8h granted migrant workers the "rights and opportunity" for a safe return.

Crucially for health rights activists, the law defined "protection" of migrant workers in terms that encompassed fulfilment of their right to health services (see Article 1(4)). To be sure, critics of the law argued that such provisions—and others in the law—did not acknowledge the full complement of migrant workers' rights (Abby and Gevani 2009, 264). But, as Taylor-Nicholson (2013) has noted, these provisions represented a significant improvement in terms of rights protection on previous policy frameworks. According to Susanti (2008, 252), the Nunukan lawsuit also appears to have had the effect of pushing along—albeit slowly—moves within the Indonesian government to ratify the UN convention on migrant workers. The government finally ratified this convention in April 2012.

In sum, then, litigation invoking the right to health (specifically the new constitutional right to obtain health services and the associated state obligation to provide health-service facilities) had a positive impact in the Nunukan migrant workers case. While the case was thrown out on appeal, it served to precipitate policy changes enhancing protection of migrant workers' rights including the right to health services. At the same time, however, this outcome was contingent upon: the very limited access to individual mechanisms through which migrant workers could

> *Litigation invoking the right to health had a positive impact in the Nunukan migrant workers case*

pursue their rights through the court system, necessitating a collective response; the difficulties of lodging class actions in Indonesia; the willingness and ability of NGO activists to mobilize the technical and financial resources required to take the migrants case to court, as well as their ingenuity in identifying the citizen lawsuit as an appropriate form of legal action; the development of an effective alliance between these activists and migrant workers groups, public figures, and ordinary citizens, which enabled the conduct of a public campaign alongside the legal action; and a considerable degree of judicial activism on the part of judges at the Central Jakarta District Court. In this respect, while the Nunukan migrant workers case illustrates the progressive potential of health rights litigation, it also illustrates the contingent nature of this potential.

Case 2: Hospital Corporatization in Jakarta

Indonesia has an extensive network of public hospitals, some of which are owned and run by the central government (these are known as Rumah Sakit Umum Pemerintah, RSUP) and some of which are owned and run by regional (i.e., district and provincial-level) governments (these are known as Rumah Sakit Umum Daerah, RSUD).[32]

Since the early 1980s, the overall proportion of these hospitals in the provision of health services has declined somewhat, as the central government has encouraged the growth of privately owned, including foreign-owned, hospitals in order to meet growing demand for hospital services (Sulastomo 1981, 128; Gani 1996, 279–80; World Bank 2008, 31).

But public hospitals have nevertheless remained important providers of hospital services, particularly to the poor and lower middle classes. For instance, according to the Ministry of Health (2014, Annex 2.6), public hospitals accounted for 34 percent of all general hospitals and 46 percent of all general hospital beds in Indonesia in 2013.[33] Public hospitals are also key pillars of the post-2014 JKN. The cost of running public hospitals has accordingly been a continual challenge for successive Indonesian governments, particularly within the context of consistently low overall government spending on health.[34] This has led to a series of policy initiatives to give public hospitals greater financial and managerial autonomy—that is, to increase the extent to which they operate like private-sector corporations on a for-profit basis.

The first major move in this direction was the New Order's introduction of the Unit Swadana (literally: self-financing bureaucratic unit) scheme in 1991. This scheme gave a group of RSUP and RSUD—then formally "unit pelaksana teknis" (UPT, technical implementation units) within the central government and regional government bureaucracies respectively—greater ability to generate, retain, and utilize income and reduce costs. The Unit Swadana mechanism also required them to provide affordable services to the poor through cross-subsidization (Gani 1996, 285). This policy lasted until 1997 when new legislation on non-tax revenues required all such revenues generated by central government entities to be transferred to the state treasury rather than being retained at the unit level. This made it impossible for RSUP to continue operating on a financially autonomous basis (Herliana 2005).

A second move towards corporatization came in 2000–2001, when the government of then President Abdurrahman Wahid decided to a) transform RSUP into *perjan*, a type of state-owned enterprise (SOE) that is wholly government-owned, concerned with the public good, and not-for-profit in orientation;[35] and b) permit regional governments to transform RSUD into regional SOEs (badan usaha milik daerah, BUMD).[36] The first of these policies ran aground as a result of subsequent legislative change through a new statute on SOEs in 2003.[37] This legislation only recognized two types of SOEs, both of which were profit-oriented: limited liability companies (perseroan terbatas, PTs), a form of SOE that could be privatized down to 51 percent government ownership; and general companies (*perum*), which were required to remain under full government ownership (Herliana 2005). The regulations on the transformation of RSUDs survived, however, creating an opportunity for regional governments to turn their RSUDs into BUMDs, including in the form of limited liability companies.[38]

In this context, the Jakarta city government announced in 2004 that it would convert three RSUDs—Pasar Rebo, Cengakareng, and Haji Hospitals—into limited liability companies. It explained that this change was necessary to improve management and services at the three hospitals and relieve pressure on the city government's budget. In August 2004, the Jakarta city parliament approved this decision, passing three regional bylaws that gave effect to the change of legal status (*Kompas* 2004a; 2004c; *Jakarta Post* 2005b).

The move was met with condemnation from staff working at the hospitals—particularly those who were civil servants—and members of local communities who relied on the hospitals for medical services (*Kompas* 2004b). For staff, the concern was that corporatization entailed a hierarchical downgrading in their status from civil servants to workers (*karyawan*) and, with that, a potential loss of job security as well as benefits such as pension entitlements (*Gatra* 2005). Members of the local community, for their part, were worried that corporatization would make hospital services more expensive, placing them out of the reach of the poorest sections of the community (*Forum Keadilan* 2005). Pasar Rebo Hospital in East Jakarta became a particular focus of resistance—possibly because it had a larger number of civil servant doctors than the other two hospitals.[39]

In January 2005, a range of local organizations—including the Pasar Rebo Hospital Workers Association, the Pasar Rebo branch of the Partai Demokrasi Indonesia-Perjuangan (PDI-P, Indonesian Democratic Party of Struggle), and various youth, student, and citizen groups—formed the Forum Rakyat Peduli Kesehatan (FRPK, Forum for People Concerned About Health). The group's aim was to provide a collective vehicle through which to protest the changes, particularly at Pasar Rebo Hospital. The FRPK organized demonstrations, initiated public discussions, lobbied the Jakarta city parliament, held press conferences, and supported legal action.[40] In May 2005, doctors at Pasar Rebo Hospital held a strike, bringing medical services to a halt and attracting widespread media attention (*Tempo Interaktif* 2005b; *Kompas* 2005c).

The move to corporatize the three public hospitals was also met with condemnation from academic public health experts such as the University of Indonesia's Hasbullah Thabrany. In a series of media comments and an academic paper, he argued that "privatization" of the three hospitals represented a breach of citizens' rights to health services and an abrogation of the state's responsibility to provide these services (*Kompas* 2004d; *Gatra* 2005; Thabrany 2005).

More crucially, Health Minister Siti Fadillah Supari condemned the move—ostensibly on ideological grounds. In media interviews she argued that transforming public hospitals into profit-seeking entities breached their social function (*Gatra* 2005; *Forum Keadilan* 2005; *Tempo Interaktif* 2005c). She lobbied President Yudhoyono to secure his support for opposing the change in legal status, apparently to good effect (*Tempo Interaktif* 2005a). In mid-February 2005, the Ministry of Home Affairs sent a letter to the Jakarta city administration stating that the corporatization of the three hospitals was "against the public interest" and requesting that it resume control of them (*Jakarta Post* 2005a). Subsequently, Supari recommended that all public hospitals should be turned into *badan layanan umum* (BLU, public service bodies), a type of bureaucratic entity with a public mission and a level of financial autonomy similar to Unit Swadana (*Tempo Interaktif* 2005c). BLUs were provided for under Law 1/2004 on the State Treasury.

> *She argued that transforming public hospitals into profit-seeking entities breached their social function*

But the then-governor of Jakarta, Sutiyoso, a keen supporter of hospital corporatization, refused to cede ground. He argued that his government's bylaws could only be overturned by a presidential decree or a Supreme Court ruling (*Kompas* 2005a; 2005b; *Jakarta Post* 2005b). He also revealed that three other Jakarta hospitals were slated for corporatization. After meeting with then–Vice President Jusuf Kalla in late March 2005, he claimed that the central government's position had now changed to one of supporting corporatization (*Jakarta Post* 2005c).

It was in the midst of these developments that doctors at Pasar Rebo Hospital and members of the local community around the hospital approached various NGOs to ask for their assistance in pursuing matters through the courts.[41] The latter agreed, and on February 5, 2005, a group of individuals representing YLKI, Yayasan Lembaga Pemberdayaan Konsumen Kesehatan Indonesia (YLPKKI, Indonesian Health Consumers Empowerment Foundation; see Table 1), and the Jakarta Consumers Foundation (an NGO with a mission similar to YLKI), as well as clients of the three hospitals,[42] lodged a request for judicial review with the Supreme Court (Mahkamah Agung 2005, 1–6). In their submission, they asked the Supreme Court to strike down the three bylaws providing for corporatization of the three hospitals on the grounds that they breached the 1945 constitution, the 1992 Health Law, and the 2004 Law on Regional Government. With regards to the 1945 constitution, they argued that hospital corporatization breached citizens' rights to obtain health services and the state's obligation to provide health-service facilities. In terms of the 1992 Health Law, they insisted that hospital corporatization is inconsistent with the government's role in providing "equitable" and "accessible" health "efforts." Finally, in relation to the 2004 Law on Regional Government, they maintained that hospital corporatization was inconsistent with regional governments' obligation to provide health-service facilities at the local level (Mahkamah Agung 2005, 14).

This move proved successful. In February 2006, the Supreme Court found in favor of the plaintiffs (although, as is common, the decision was not announced until a few months later; *Kompas* 2006a).[43] The Supreme Court did not rule on the constitutionality of the bylaws, noting that this was not within its authority (indeed, only the Constitutional Court can rule on constitutional breaches, but it is limited to reviewing the constitutionality of statutes). However, the Supreme Court ruled that the three bylaws were inconsistent with the 1992 Health Law and the 2004 Law on Regional Government; determined that the bylaws were thus invalid; and instructed the Jakarta city administration to withdraw them (Mahkamah Agung 2005, 31).

Given the health minister's position on the issue and the president's apparent support for her position, this decision was perhaps less clearly an instance of judicial activism than the one made by the Jakarta District Court in the Nunukan migrant workers case. But it can be regarded as such to the extent that it challenged the powerful interests within the Jakarta city administration that had pushed for hospital corporatization.

Because enforcement of the ruling lay with the Jakarta city administration, the latter had the option of ignoring the court's ruling and proceeding with the change of status. But, in the face of public opposition to the bylaws, Sutiyoso announced that his government would comply with the ruling and, in August 2006, the city parliament voted to withdraw the bylaws (*Jakarta Post* 2006; *Kompas* 2006b). Over the course of the next couple of years, all three hospitals were converted to BLU.

As in the Nunukan migrant workers case, therefore, litigation invoking the right to health had a progressive impact to the extent that it precipitated policy change which enhanced access to health services for the poor and marginalized. But, once again, this outcome was contingent upon a set of particular preconditions. Similar to the Nunukan case, these included the existence of an available legal pathway for challenging the Jakarta city administration's bylaws (in the form of the Supreme Court's judicial review process); the willingness and ability of NGO activists to mobilize the technical and financial resources required to take matters to court; the development of an effective alliance between these activists, the media, and the doctors and local community around Pasar Rebo Hospital; and a significant degree of judicial activism on the part of judges at (in this case) the Supreme Court. Favorable preconditions also included state responsiveness, in the form of active support from the health minister (for whom, it would seem, the case presented an opportunity to assert her radical populist credentials) to litigation demands.

Case 3: The BPJS Law

The early post–New Order period witnessed a series of moves to improve the country's social security system and, in particular, ensure that

Indonesian citizens had access to health insurance. These included, as noted earlier, the incorporation of an article into the 1945 constitution providing citizens with a right to social security (Article 28H (3)); the introduction of various national and regional schemes providing free health insurance to the poor and/or near poor (e.g., ASKESKIN and JAMKESMAS); and the enactment of Law 40/2004 on Social Security. The latter was particularly important because "it was the first ever legislation ruling that all Indonesians [would] be covered by social security through five mandatory universal programs—healthcare benefits, occupational accident benefits, old-age risk benefits, pension benefits and death benefits" (Tjandra 2014, 9). However, this envisaged set of social insurance schemes could not be fully implemented until an ancillary law on BPJS was enacted.

Law 40/2004 provided a definition of BPJS, saying that they would be "legal entities that are formed to implement social security programs" (Article 1(6)). In the preamble to the law's elucidation, it was also stated that these organizations would constitute a "transformation" of the SOEs that then managed the social security system (i.e., PT TASPEN, PT ASKES, PT ASABRI, and PT JAMSOSTEK). Furthermore, the law specified some general principles that would govern the new system—

The new system would operate on a not-for-profit basis and social security funds would be held in trust

for instance, it would operate on a not-for-profit basis and social security funds would be held in trust. But beyond this, it said little about the legal status, responsibilities, and orientation of the BPJS organizations and how they would operate. This rendered much of Law 40/2004 un-implementable. The law specified that a new law on the establishment and operation of the various BPJS components should be enacted within five years of the passage of Law 40/2004—that is, by October 19, 2009. However, by that deadline—which coincided with the beginning of Yudhoyono's second term—the government had not submitted draft legislation to the national parliament, let alone secured its enactment.

The introduction of a new law on BPJS ran up against stern opposition from a range of powerful actors. These included the social security SOEs mentioned above, the Indonesian business community (especially Asosiasi Pengusaha Indonesia, APINDO, the Indonesian Employers Association), and senior echelons of government. Some politico-bureaucratic and corporate elites feared that they would lose control over social security funds, which were a key source of funds for both strategic government initiatives and rents for government officials, well-connected business groups, and senior officials in the social security SOEs. Other government leaders, including Yudhoyono himself, dragged their feet on the BPJS legislation out of concern about the fiscal impact of the new social security system (Wisnu 2012, 95–164). Some opposition also emerged from the trade union movement, with leading unionists arguing that the state should provide services for free, rather than asking workers to pay for them through premiums. Additionally, Tjandra (2014, 14) has suggested that this union opposition was partly due to the fact that some trade unions sat on the board of and received financial support from PT JAMSOSTEK and that they therefore enjoyed access to its resources and rents. However, as this study will address below, the majority of trade unions supported the law.

In this context, activists at Prakarsa (see Table 1) prepared a draft bill on the BPJS and secured the support of the PDI-P to submit it for deliberation as part of the DPR's 2010 legislative program. (PDI-P's leader, Megawati Sukarnoputri, had signed off on Law 40/2004 on her last day as president in 2004 and was, consequently, favorably disposed towards the necessary follow-up legislation.) This put pressure on the government to engage in negotiations with the DPR over the bill, although the government was able to delay the bill's progress with debate over minutiae and by refusing to make compromises.

At the same time, dozens of trade unions, NGOs, student organizations, professional bodies, and other organizations formed the Komite Aksi Jaminan Sosial (KAJS, Action Committee for Social Security) to lead a popular campaign to promote passing of the bill. In April and May 2010, KAJS organized demonstrations across the country that involved tens of thousands of people, most of whom were labor activists. These protests demanded the quick endorsement and subsequent enactment of the BPJS bill and, with that, healthcare and pensions for all Indonesians as well as the transformation of the social security SOEs into trusts (Tjandra 2014, 10–11).

In June 2010, KAJS then lodged a citizen lawsuit at the Central Jakarta District Court aimed at forcing the government and parliament to pass the bill. The lawsuit listed 120 individuals, mostly trade union activists, as plaintiffs, and it was supported by a legal team under the leadership of Surya Tjandra from TURC. As in the Nunukan and hospital corporatization cases, the lawyers involved in the court case all provided their assistance and expertise pro bono.[44] The lawsuit centered on a claim that, by failing to pass and enact the new law on BPJS, the government had committed illegal acts—in particular, breaching provisions of the 1945 constitution, of the 1999 Human Rights Law, and of Law 40/2004 as well as other legislation providing citizens with a right to social security.

At the same time, the KAJS also made reference to the state's constitutional obligation to provide health-service facilities as part of its argument that "health insurance was a basic need that must be fulfilled by the State for all Indonesian people without exception and for the full term of people's lives (*universal coverage*)" (italics in original; Action Committee for Social Security 2010, 27). While some of these arguments were likely to be rejected on the grounds that the court had no authority to rule on breaches of the constitution, the government's failure to produce and pass a BPJS law by 2009 offered a good chance that the judges would find the executive in violation of Law 40/2004.

To pressure the court into finding in its favor, the KAJS sought media attention for the case and organized a series of demonstrations both inside and outside the court (Tjandra 2014, 11–12). This approach proved successful.

In July 2011, the Central Jakarta District Court found for the plaintiffs, declaring that—indeed—the government had been negligent in implementing Law 40/2004. It therefore instructed the executive to enact a new law on BPJS and produce various accompanying regulations (Pengadilan Negeri Jakarta Pusat 2011, 243). Given the reluctance of the government to pass the BPJS law, this was a bold move and a clear act of judicial activism. The government immediately appealed the decision to the Jakarta High Court but the decision of the court of first instance nevertheless applied further pressure on the government and parliament to pass and enact the BPJS law.

In October 2011, the KAJS mobilized workers, students, farmers, and other social groups for some of the largest demonstrations ever seen outside the national parliament as a technical deadline for passage of the draft legislation loomed (Tjandra 2014, 13). Faced with a court instruction and such enormous mass pressure, the parliament and government eventually passed the new law on October 28.

This decision did not fully end matters, however. There were two reasons for this.

First, shortly after the KAJS had lodged the citizen lawsuit in June 2010, individuals associated with the DKR, the Serikat Rakyat Miskin Indonesia (SRMI; see Table 1), and a separate set of trade unions had lodged a judicial review case with the Constitutional Court aimed at annulling key parts of Law 40/2004. As in the other cases examined here, these individuals were supported by a pro bono legal team—in this case, based at the DKR.[45] Whereas the KAJS pragmatically aimed to lock in Law 40/2004 on the grounds that it provided for a social security system that was better than before, these individuals took a more idealistic position. They belonged to a group of unions that, as indicated earlier, rejected Law 40/2004 because it required workers to pay premiums to the state in order to obtain social security. In their view, by contrast, the 1945 constitution envisaged a social security system fully funded by government. In their legal arguments, the plaintiffs focused on breaches of provisions in the 1945 constitution related to social security (Mahkamah Konstitutsi 2011a). In addition, their star witness, former Health Minister Siti Fadillah Supari, also invoked the constitutional right to obtain health services: the requirement to pay premiums, she argued, "could be understood as meaning that those who do not pay do not have the right to health services provided by government" (Mahkamah Konstitutsi 2011b, 14).

> *The 1945 constitution imposed an obligation on the state to fund social security for the poor*

If successful, this case would have rendered crucial sections of both Law 40/2004 and the proposed BPJS law invalid, a move that, in the eyes of KAJS activists, would have set back the social security cause for decades.[46] In late November 2011, however, the Constitutional Court rejected the DKR/SRMI submission, ruling that the 1945 constitution did not prohibit a social security system in which workers paid premiums; it merely imposed an obligation on the state to fund social security for the poor (Mahkamah Konstitusi 2011a, 92). In making this decision, the Constitutional Court thus fell into line with the earlier decision of the Central Jakarta District Court and the deal brokered between the parliament and the government in October 2011. Four days later, President Susilo Bambang Yudhoyono signed the BPJS law, concluding the enactment process.

The second complication in bringing the BPJS law to implementation was the fact that the Jakarta High Court had still not ruled on the government's appeal in relation to the citizen lawsuit. In December 2012, roughly one year after enactment of the BPJS law, it finally did so. In contrast to the Central Jakarta District Court, it found that it had no authority to instruct the government to enact a law. The power to determine whether laws were needed, it said, rested solely with the DPR and government. It accordingly overturned the Central Jakarta District Court's decision in its entirety (Pengadilan Tinggi Jakarta 2012). This appeal outcome had no influence on the status of the BPJS law, however, because it came too late to influence the parliament's decision to enact the BPJS law. Thus, the BPJS law was implemented, leading to—among other things—the beginning of JKN operations in early 2014.

As in the two previous cases, litigation invoking the right to health—in this case in the form of the right to social security as well as the right to obtain health services—had a progressive impact to the extent that it served to precipitate policy change that enhanced protection of citizens' right to access such services. Similar to the other cases, this outcome was contingent upon particular preconditions, namely: the availability of legal pathways for challenging government actions/inaction; the willingness and ability of NGO activists to mobilize the technical and financial resources required to take matters to court; the development of an effective alliance between these activists and subordinate forces (in this case organized labor, student organizations, and various other social groups); and state responsiveness in the form of judicial activism. Furthermore, the case also illustrates how the right to health can be harnessed to competing progressive agendas: for instance, to both the pragmatic platform of the KAJS and the more radical agenda of the DKR and SRMI. In this respect, the BPJS case shows that the effect of the right to health depends in no small respect on which actor takes the initiative to claim it and for what broader socio-political purpose this initiative is pursued.

Case 4: The Central Government's Health Budget

Indonesian government spending on health has long been low by international standards (see Figure 1). Underlying this low level of spending has been the continued political dominance throughout the New Order and post–New Order periods of predatory military and bureaucratic officials, well-connected business groups, and liberal technocrats. These elements have sought to limit government spending on social policy programs—including those related to health—for a variety of reasons. Liberal technocrats, for instance, fear that high spending on government-funded health care could undermine Indonesia's macroeconomic stability. Predatory elites and well-connected business groups, on the other hand, are keen to channel resources for government spending into areas closer to their interests.

Following the fall of the New Order, donor organizations such as the World Bank and the United Nations Children's Fund (UNICEF), the Ikatan Dokter Indonesia (IDI, Indonesian Doctors' Association), various public health intellectuals, and several NGOs began to openly call for increased public health spending. They argued that this, quite obviously, was necessary to improve health outcomes (*Kompas* 2000; 2003; Andang 2008; Bahagijo 2009, World Bank 2009a). This move—combined with the incentives created by democratization for political elites to adopt populist policies—yielded new commitments to increase public health spending in the run-up to elections (*Kompas* 2004b; Vivanews 2009). It also led to the DPR's decision to include in the 2009 Health Law a requirement for the central government to spend at least 5 percent of its budget on health-related expenses excluding salaries and wages (Article 171 (1)).

However, while central government spending on health increased during the 2000s and early 2010s, it consistently fell well short of the 5 percent target, peaking at 3.6 percent of total government spending in 2011 (Mahkamah Konstitusi 2012, 31). In this context, a group of organizations and individuals led by Prakarsa, the Indonesian Human Rights Committee For Social Justice (IHCS), and the Forum Indonesia untuk Transparansi Anggaran (FITRA, the Indonesian Forum for Budget Transparency; see Table 1) lodged a request for judicial

Figure 1. Public Health Expenditures
(as a percentage of gross domestic product)

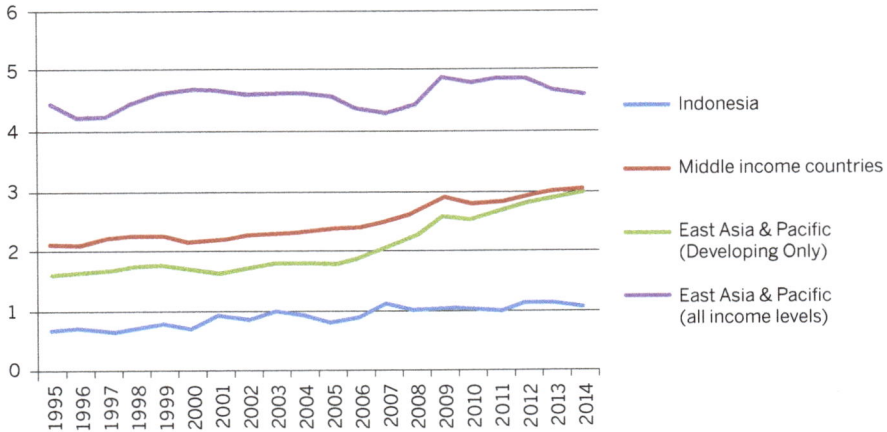

Source: World Bank, World Development Indicators database.

review with the Constitutional Court. The plaintiffs challenged the law on the 2010 budget on the grounds that it breached the 1945 constitution by, among other things, allocating insufficient funds to health (that is, less than 5 percent of the total budget). The plaintiffs were supported by a team of lawyers based at IHCS who offered their services pro bono. One year later, they lodged a similar request for judicial review with the Constitutional Court, challenging the legislation on the 2011 budget as well.

In both cases, they argued, in allocating less than 5 percent of the central government budget to health, the budget laws breached Articles 28H (1) and 34 (3) of the 1945 constitution—the provisions providing citizens with a right to obtain health services and imposing an obligation on the state to provide health-service facilities respectively (Mahkamah Konstitusi 2011c; 2012). In legal terms, their case was similar to earlier successful Constitutional Court challenges brought between 2005 and 2008 by the Indonesian teachers union (PGRI) and other NGOs against previous budget laws that allocated less than 20 percent of the total central government budget to education. However, it was weaker to the extent that the 1945 constitution explicitly requires governments at all levels to spend 20 percent of their respective budgets on education but specifies no minimum spending for either the central government or regional governments on health.

According to Yuna Farhan (2012, xv), the secretary-general of FITRA, the purpose of the judicial review was "to raise awareness within Indonesian society about citizens' constitutional right to challenge budgets managed by the state." Yet it does not appear to have been successful in this respect, at least not in terms of having an immediate impact. In contrast to the other cases examined in this study, the court case attracted little media attention and stimulated no broader popular mobilization.

> *In contrast, this court case attracted little media attention and stimulated no broader popular mobilization*

This was notwithstanding the fact that, as noted earlier, a range of actors had publically expressed support for increased public health spending. The reasons for this failure to attract media attention and generate broad popular mobilization are unclear but probably include: a) the unwillingness or inability of key actors such as the IDI and foreign donors to openly challenge government policy[47] and b) the fact that the country's trade unions—groups with the clear ability to mobilize large numbers of people—were heavily engaged at the time in the struggle over the implementation of Law 40/2004 and may, in any case, have felt that the health budget was less relevant to their interests. Whatever the reason, there was clearly less pressure from the media and popular forces on the court to find in favor of the plaintiffs than in the other three cases examined here.

Facing little public pressure, the Constitutional Court found against the NGOs and their allies. Under the 1945 constitution, it determined, the state is only obliged "to make a real effort" (*mengupayakan secara sungguh-sungguh*) to fulfil citizens' health needs and provide adequate health services, not to ensure that all citizens are healthy (Mahkamah Konstitusi 2011c, 13–14).

But while the court case did not impact the policy of the incumbent Yudhoyono government—which did not pass health budgets reaching 5 percent of the total budget in its ten years in office—it may have influenced Yudhoyono's successor, Joko Widodo (or Jokowi), to take a different approach. Although the health budget remained below 5 percent in 2015—the first full year of Jokowi's rule—it passed this threshold in 2016 when it increased 43 percent over the previous year and constituted 5.05 percent of the total budget (Aditiasari 2015; *Geotimes* 2015). The 2017 budget was also designed in a way to exceed the 5 percent level—although some critics have challenged the government's mechanism of calculating its allocations, which include transfers to the regions (Ministry of Finance n.d.). But whatever the exact basis for arriving at the total volume of the health budget, the Jokowi government clearly believed that formally meeting the 5 percent requirement was important. The possibility of further lawsuits—similar to the 2010 and 2011 cases—might have played a role in their coming to that conclusion.

In this case, then, the transformative potential of health rights litigation did not translate into immediate outcomes. It seems, however, to have contributed to the opinion building among political leaders who, when they came to office several years later, implemented what the court in 2011 had rejected as not constitutionally mandatory. The 2011 defeat in the court, and the unwillingness of the then government to act on the demands of the plaintiffs, was partly due to apparent weaknesses in the legal case being advanced. But it was also in part because of a lack of media and popular pressure, which meant that the Constitutional Court had more political room to maneuver and less incentive to engage in judicial activism than in the other cases examined here. The lack of public pressure, media attention, and judicial activism notwithstanding, the plaintiffs saw their demand met years later, pointing once more to the role of health litigation in—at the very least—putting important issues on the agenda and in creating an environment in which such demands can be effectively pursued.

Conclusion: Comparative and Policy Implications

This study has examined the impact of health rights litigation in Indonesia as well as the political and social factors that have shaped it. Analysis has shown that health rights litigation has had progressive effects in that such litigation has precipitated policy changes consistent with the fulfilment of the right to health for poor and marginalized citizens.

Moreover, the discussion of several case studies highlighted that this outcome has been contingent upon: a) the presence of judicial and health institutions that have simultaneously limited the scope for citizens to engage in individually focused litigation while enabling them to engage in collectively focused litigation; b) enhanced elite (including judicial) responsiveness to social policy concerns as a result of the combined effects of the Asian economic crisis and democratization; and c) the fact that the country has had a cohort of NGOs that have been committed to the right to health, had the financial and technical resources to mobilize the law, and possessed the ability to forge alliances with and mobilize popular forces.

In so doing, the discussion has demonstrated that the effects of health rights litigation have depended not simply on whether litigation has been individually or collectively focused—the variable emphasized by Brinks and Gauri (2014). The impact of such litigation has also depended on variables relating to the political and social context for collectively oriented litigation, such as elite responsiveness to social policy concerns and the orientation, resources, and alliances of NGOs.

What are the implications of this analysis for efforts to promote fulfilment of the right to health in developing countries in general?

First, the analysis suggests that developing countries that have experienced high levels of individually focused health rights litigation as well as related fiscal and distributional problems need to consider institutional changes to their judicial and legal systems to promote the fulfilment of health rights. As Brinks and Gauri (2014, 388) have noted, some commentators have suggested that judicial and health systems in such countries should be redesigned so as to prevent citizens from lodging individual health rights claims through the court system altogether. This is one option.

There are, however, less blunt approaches. These entail two elements: a) the provision of legal aid to the poor so that they have the same opportunity as middle-class citizens to lodge individual health rights claims; and b) the introduction of requirements, either through the evolution of judicial doctrine or the enactment of legislation, for judges to balance the will to ensure fulfilment of individuals' health rights against concerns regarding distributional and macro-economic impacts. Applied properly, such approaches would encourage judges to facilitate access to publicly funded medicines and health services on the basis of need while, at the same time, minimizing the risk of a blowout in government health spending.

Second, the analysis suggests that health rights litigation is most likely to be effective in countries where the broader political and social environment supports the fulfilment of health rights. There are two dimensions to this.

To begin with, it is crucial that organizations such as the various NGOs involved in the four cases above exist, have the technical and legal resources to mobilize the law, and can forge alliances with and mobilize subaltern groups. In addition, key sections of the elite (including the judiciary) need to be supportive of the right to health.

> *It is crucial that organizations have the technical and legal resources to mobilize the law, forge alliances, and mobilize subaltern groups*

Neither of these conditions can be taken for granted. NGOs often have precarious funding bases while political and judicial elites operate within the context of regimes providing different incentives and disincentives vis-à-vis responsiveness to social policy concerns. Even in democratic contexts, these elites may have alternative strategies for mobilizing popular support—for instance, building party machines and cultivating patronage networks.[48]

It is difficult for supporters of health rights—whether domestic or international—to successfully manufacture these two noted conditions. But both domestic actors and international donors can certainly help by, for example, providing financial support to the relevant NGOs to ensure that they retain the financial and technical resources needed to mobilize the law and build alliances.

Finally, the analysis suggests that health rights litigation is most effective when supported by political mobilization. Much analysis, particularly that associated with the "law and social movements" literature (e.g., Scheingold 1974; Rosenberg 1991), has proposed that legal mobilization is often ineffective as a strategy for rights activists because courts are aligned with the status quo and, hence, tend to be unsympathetic to rights-related causes (although some scholars have shown that legal mobilization can serve to build movement cohesion and capacity; McCann 1994). Skeptics of legal mobilization have consequently argued that rights activists should instead focus on engaging in political mobilization. This study, in contrast, suggests that legal and political mobilization should not be considered as discrete, mutually exclusive options for promoting health rights but as components of a unified strategy. That is, they can be effective *when they go hand-in-hand with one another.*

In strategic terms, the implication is that NGOs with the technical capacity and financial resources to launch legal action need to forge links to groups with deep roots in society and significant influence. Such alliances help to maximize capacity to attract media attention, hold protests, and engage in other forms of political mobilization in order to produce effective activism in favor of the right to health.

Overall, then, the analysis here suggests that concerned individuals should neither be excessively optimistic nor overly dismissive regarding the transformative potential of health rights litigation. Such potential exists but realizing it is not straightforward—to have an impact, health litigation initiatives need to coincide with numerous other factors supportive of better health policy.

In this context, it is important to note that notwithstanding the judicial decisions made in the case studies analyzed above, Indonesia's health system continues to be widely criticized for its poor quality and ineffectiveness in addressing key health challenges such as maternal mortality and HIV/AIDS (Amnesty International 2010; UNICEF Indonesia 2012; Dwicaksono and Setiawan 2013). Transforming Indonesia's new health rights-in-law into the fulfilment of health rights-in-practice will require ongoing political and social struggle over an extended period of time. So will similar changes in other developing countries. This struggle will need to occur outside the courts as much as within them—and, indeed, must do so if it is to be effective.

Endnotes

1. For analyses of other developing countries' experiences with health rights litigation, see Gauri and Brinks (2008), Gloppen (2008), and Yamin and Gloppen (2011).

2. In the former case, litigation combined with human rights advocacy yielded reductions in the price of HIV/AIDs medication and in additional resources for the health system and the poor (Heywood 2013). In the latter case, Indian Supreme Court decisions establishing a right to health provided the legal basis for a series of subsequent judicial decisions upholding the state's obligation to maintain health services and otherwise fulfil the right to health. These judicial decisions, in turn, placed pressure on the Indian government to change its policies and implement practices promoting the fulfilment of health rights (Singh, Govender, and Mills 2007).

3. This definition reproduces in large part that advanced by Gloppen and Roseman (2011, 4). But it is different in two respects. First, it includes litigation based on state obligations associated with the right to health or related rights. Second, it includes litigation where the relevant rights or obligations are provided for in laws as well as in the constitution.

4. *Amparo* was introduced originally in Mexico in the 1800s but has since spread throughout Latin America and to some other parts of the world. In its many forms, it "allows citizens to bring an action in court against the government for a violation of fundamental or constitutional rights. It is meant to be restorative as opposed to compensatory, and is a means of providing relatively immediate relief in otherwise overloaded and slow judicial systems" (Miguel-Stearns 2015).

5. As is discussed following, the only court with the authority to rule on matters of constitutionality is the Constitutional Court. Its authority in this respect, however, has been strictly circumscribed to dealing with issues of consistency between the 1945 constitution and laws. State administrative courts (pengadilan tata usaha negara, PTUN) have authority to resolve disputes over administrative matters,

including ones related to the consistency between administrative decisions and higher-level laws and regulations. However, as Bedner (2008, 236) has noted, their jurisdiction has been tightly circumscribed by the Supreme Court.

6. Under the government's road map for the JKN, the scheme is to be fully rolled out by 2019 (National Team for the Acceleration of Poverty Reduction 2015).

7. According to Ramesh (2014, 43), JAMSOSTEK's health insurance program only covered 6 percent of formal private-sector workers in 2010, in large part because of widespread evasion and poor enforcement. This was despite the fact that the program was formally mandatory.

8. According to Tempo.co (2016), the JKN only provided coverage to two-thirds of the Indonesian population in October 2016. For the most part, the shortfall in coverage has been due to difficulties in incorporating informal private-sector workers. But it has also been due, in part, to the difficulties getting private businesses to enrol employees in the scheme (see Jong 2015).

9. For a discussion of the powers of the Constitutional Court, see Asshiddiqie (2006) and Butt (2015).

10. Interview, Gatot Goei, former YLBHI activist, May 2013.

11. Social welfare insurance (Asuransi Kesejahteraan Sosial, ASKESOS), an income replacement scheme for informal private-sector workers, was trialled between 1996 and 1998 but not fully implemented until the 2000s. Even then it only provided support to a small number of people (Rosser and van Diermen 2016).

12. For an analysis of the radical populist tradition in Indonesia's economic thinking, see Chalmers and Hadiz (1997, Chs. 5 and 8).

13. Interviews, World Bank, WHO, and Australian Department of Foreign Affairs and Trade officials, November 2013 and November 2015.

14. Interview, World Bank official, Jakarta, November 2015.

15. The term "judicial activism" has been used in a wide variety of ways (see Kmiec 2004 for an extended discussion). It is used here to refer to judicial actions that promote human rights in the face of powerful elite opposition.

16. Interview, Tulus Abadi, YLKI activist, Jakarta, November 2013.

17. Interview, an informed source, Jakarta, June 2009.

18. Interview, Ade Irawan and Febri Hendri, ICW activists, Jakarta, June 2009.

19. See http://www.mantabs.com/pages/56_about_us.

20. Interview, Marius Widjajarta, Jakarta, November 2015.

21. Interview, Sri Palupi, Jakarta, August 2014.

22. Interview, Ah Maftuchan, Director of Prakarsa, Jakarta, November 2015.

23. ibid.

24. Interview, Surya Tjandra, Jakarta, November 2015.

25. Interview, IHCS activists, Jakarta, November 2015.

26. Interview, Weby Warouw, DKR activist, November 2009.

27. Interview, Surya Tjandra, Jakarta, November 2015.

28. Interview, Dinna Wisnu, Jakarta, November 2015.

29. Interview, Sri Palupi, Institute for Ecosoc Rights, Jakarta, November 2014.

30. Surya Tjandra, one of the lawyers involved in the lawsuit. Personal communication, July 2016.

31. ibid.

32. For the purposes of this study, the term "public hospitals" does not include central-government-owned SOEs (badan usaha milik negara, BUMN) and hospitals owned by ministries other than the Ministry of Health.

33. These figures do not include general hospitals owned by the army, police, state-owned enterprises, and ministries other than the Ministry of Health. These hospitals tend to operate like private hospitals.

34. On the government's health budget, see the final case study.

35. *Perjan* were distinguished from other types of SOEs on the grounds that they had to be wholly state-owned and "promote the public good through the provision of high quality public services without just seeking profits." See Articles 1 and 2 of Presidential Regulation 6/2000 on *Perusahaan Jawatan*.

36. See Presidential Decree 40/2001 on Guidelines for the Institutionalisation and Management of Regional Hospitals.

37. See Law 19/2003 on State-Owned Enterprises.

38. New legislation on regional governments in 2003 stated that regional governments should include "regional technical units" (RTUs) and these in turn could include RSUD. But it did not explicitly require that RSUD take the form of RTUs.

39. Interview, Anis Saduk, head of the Forum Rakyat Peduli Kesehatan (FRPK), Jakarta, November 2015.

40. See http://panjioposisi.blogspot.com.au/2008/07/forum-rakyat-peduli-kesehatan
.html. See also http://news.detik.com/read/2006/01/25/124909/525971/10/dinilai-
gagal-privatisasi-rsud-diminta-distop?nd992203605, accessed November 7, 2014.

41. Interviews, Marius Widjajarta and Anis Saduk, both Jakarta and both November
2015.

42. These included a patient at Pasar Rebo Hospital, a patient at Haji Hospital, and
the parent of a patient at Pasar Rebo Hospital.

43. In this context, the term plaintiff equates to *pemohon* (literally, requestor) rather
than *penggugat* (literally, accuser) because the parties filed for judicial review rather than a civil lawsuit.

44. Interview, Surya Tjandra, August 2014.

45. Interview, Tutut Herlina, a DKR activist involved in the court case, Jakarta,
August 2014.

46. Interview, Surya Tjandra, Jakarta, August 2014.

47. During the New Order, the professional medical organizations—of which IDI
is the most prominent—were subordinated to and closely integrated with the
Ministry of Health. As such, they acted as mechanisms for political control, rev-
enue mobilization, and patronage distribution rather than the articulation of
bottom-up concerns about policy and the fulfilment of human rights. As Murphy
(2008, 20) has noted, the New Order used its authority to license professionals (including medical professionals) as a way to "silence dissent" and it "often
intervened directly in the affairs of professional organizations by installing loyal
Golkar functionaries in leadership positions." Following the collapse of the New
Order and transition to democracy in the late 1990s, the professional medical
organizations—and IDI in particular—have remained deeply integrated with the
health bureaucracy, limiting their scope for promoting health rights causes. Interview with activists from United Indonesian Doctors, a splinter group within IDI,
November 2015.

48. On these strategies, see Tans (2011).

Bibliography

Abby, Tabrani, and Ariefanto Gevani. 2009. "Hukum Perburuhan." In *Panduan Bantuan Hukum di Indonesia,* edited by Agustinus Edy Kristianto, A. Patra M. Zen, and Carolina S. Martha, 229–84. Jakarta: Yayasan Obor Indonesia.

Action Committee for Social Security. 2010. *Gugatan Perbuatan Melawan Hukum Atas Penyelengaraan Jaminan Sosial,* Jakarta.

Aditiasari, Dana. 2015. "Anggaran Kesehatan 2016 Naik 43%, Ini Fokus Pemerintah," *detikFinance.* Accessed April 13, 2017, https://finance.detik.com/ekonomi-bisnis/2992640/anggaran-kesehatan-2016-naik-43-ini-fokus-pemerintah.

Al Azhari, Muhamad, and Dion Bisara. 2016. "Indonesia Ranks 14th Among Remittance Recipients: World Bank," *Jakarta Globe.* Accessed April 12, 2017, http://jakartaglobe.id/business/indonesia-ranks-14th-among-remittance-recipients-world-bank/.

Amnesty International. 2010. *Left Without a Choice: Barriers to Reproductive Health in Indonesia.* London: Amnesty International Publications.

Andang, Ilyani. 2008. "APBN Untuk Siapa?," *Kompas,* May 28.

Antlöv, Hans, Rustam Ibrahim, and Peter van Tuijl. 2006. "NGO Governance and Accountability in Indonesia: Challenges in a Newly Democratizing Country." In *NGO Accountability: Politics, Principles and Innovation,* edited by Lisa Jordan and Peter Van Tuijl, 147–162. London: Earthscan.

Aspinall, Edward. 2005. *Opposing Suharto: Compromise, Resistance and Regime Change in Indonesia.* Stanford: Stanford University Press.

Asshiddiqie, Jimly. 2006. *Hukum Acara: Pengujian Undang-undang.* Jakarta: Konstitusi Press.

Bahagijo, Sugeng. 2009. "Kesehatan Untuk Semua," *Kompas*, February 2.

Bari, S., ed. 2009. *Kumpulan Wawancara Siti Fadillah Supari: Berkiblat Kata Hati Menggeser Tapal Batas Dunia*, Yogyakarta: SFS Fans Club and Lembaga Kajian Islam, dan Sosial.

Bedner, Adriaan. 2008. "Rebuilding the Judiciary in Indonesia: The Special Courts Strategy," *Yuridika* 23 (3):230–53.

Bergallo, Paolo. 2011. "Argentina: Courts and the Right to Health: Achieving Fairness Despite 'Routinization' in Individual Coverage Cases." In *Litigating Health Rights: Can Courts Bring More Justice to Health?*, edited by Alicia Yamin and Siri Gloppen. Cambridge, MA: Harvard University Press.

Biehl, Joao, Adriana Petryna, Alex Gertner, Jospeh Amon, and Paulo Picon. 2009. "The Judicialisation of the Right to Health in Brazil," *The Lancet* 373 (9682):2182–84.

Bourchier, David. 1999. "Magic Memos, Collusion and Judges With Attitude: Notes on the Politics of Law in Contemporary Indonesia." In *Law, Capitalism and Power: The Rule of Law and Legal Institutions*, edited by Kanishka Jayasuriya, 233–52. London: Routledge.

Brinks, Daniel, and Varun Gauri. 2014. "The Law's Majestic Equality? The Distributive Impact of Judicializing Social and Economic Rights," *Perspectives on Politics* 12 (2):375–93.

Budiarti, Rita Triana. 2013. *Kontroversi Mahfud MD Jilid II: Di Balik Putusan Mahkamah Konstitusi*. Jakarta: Konstitusi Press.

Buehler, Michael. 2008. "No Positive News," *Inside Indonesia* 94: Oct.–Dec. Accessed March 7, 2016, http://www.insideindonesia.org/no-positive-news.

Butt, Simon. 2015. *The Constitutional Court and Democracy in Indonesia*. Leiden: Brill.

Butt, Simon, and Nicholas Parsons. 2014. "Judicial Review and the Supreme Court in Indonesia: A New Space for Law?," *Indonesia* 97 (April):55–85.

Chalmers, Ian, and Vedi R. Hadiz, eds. 1997. *The Politics of Economic Development in Indonesia: Contending Perspective*. London: Routledge.

Crouch, Harold. 2010. *Political Reform in Indonesia After Soeharto*. Singapore: Institute of Southeast Asian Studies.

Dwicaksono, Adenantera, and Donny Setiawan. 2013. *Monitoring Kebijakan dan Anggaran Komitmen Pemerintah Indonesia Dalam Kesehatan Ibu*. Bandung: Perkumpulan Inisiatif.

Farhan, Yuna. 2012. "Pengantar FITRA." In *Menggugat APBN: Ketika Keuangan Negara Tidak Untuk Sebesar-besarnya Kemakmuran Rakyat*, edited by Achmad Ya'kub, xv–xvi. Jakarta: IHCS and Yayasan TIFA.

Ferraz, Octavio. 2009. "The Right to Health in the Courts of Brazil: Worsening Health Inequities?," *Health and Human Rights* 11 (2):33–45.

Ferraz, Octavio. 2011. "Brazil: Health Inequalities, Rights, and Courts: The Social Impact of the Judicialization of Health." In *Litigating Health Rights: Can Courts Bring More Justice to Health?*, edited by Alicia Yamin and Siri Gloppen. Cambridge, MA: Harvard University Press.

FITRA. n.d. "Sejarah Singkat Organisasi." Accessed July 8, 2016, http://seknasfitra.org/perihal/sejarah-singkat-organisasi/.

Flood, Colleen, and Aeyal Gross. 2014. "Litigating the Right to Health: What Can We Learn from a Comparative Law and Health Care Systems Approach?," *Health and Human Rights* 16 (2):62–72.

Ford, Michele. 2006. "Migrant Worker Organizing in Indonesia," *Asian and Pacific Migration Journal* 15 (3):313–34.

Forum Keadilan. 2005. "Selamat Tinggal Rumah Sakit Miskin," March 20.

Gani, Ascobat. 1996. "Improving Quality in Public Sector Hospitals in Indonesia," *International Journal of Health Planning and Management* 11:275–96.

Gatra. 2005. "Menolak Persero Bertarif," February 5.

Gauri, Varun, and Daniel Brinks, eds. 2008. *Courting Social Justice: Judicial Enforcement of Social and Economic Rights in the Developing World*. New York: Cambridge University Press.

Geotimes. 2015. "Anggaran Kesehatan Indonesia Naik Menjadi 5 Persen," July 6. Accessed April 13, 2017, http://geotimes.co.id/anggaran-kesehatan-indonesia-naik-menjadi-5-persen/#gs.d_ESWIM.

Gloppen, Siri. 2008. "Litigation as a Strategy to Hold Governments Accountable for Implementing the Right to Health," *Health and Human Rights* 10 (2):21–36.

Gloppen, Siri, and Mindy Roseman. 2011. "Introduction: Can Litigation Bring Justice to Health?" In *Litigating Health Rights: Can Courts Bring More Justice to Health?*, edited by Alicia Yamin and Siri Gloppen, 1–16. Cambridge, MA: Harvard University Press.

Hendrianto. 2016. "The Rise and Fall of Heroic Chief Justices: Constitutional Politics and Judicial Leadership in Indonesia," *Washington International Law Journal* 25 (3):489-563.

Herliana, Elin. 2005. "Mencari Kelembagaan Ideal Rumah Sakit Pemerintah: (Privatisasi VS Nonprivatisasi)," *Kompas*, May 17.

Hermawanto. 2009. "Advokasi." In *Panduan Bantuan Hukum di Indonesia*, edited by Agustinus Edy Kristianto, A. Patra M. Zen, and Carolina S. Martha, 475–509. Jakarta: Yayasan Obor Indonesia.

Heywood, Mark. 2013. "South Africa's Treatment Action Campaign: Combining Law and Social Mobilization to Realize the Right to Health," *Journal of Human Rights Practice* 1 (1):14–36.

Holliday, Ian. 2000. "Productivist Welfare Capitalism: Social Policy in East Asia," *Political Studies* 48 (4):706–23.

Hukum Online. 2003. "Pro-kontra Citizen Law Suit: Belajar dari Kasus Nunukan," May 14. Accessed July 8, 2016, http://www.hukumonline.com/berita /baca/hol8003/prokontra-citizenlaw-suit-belaiar-dari-kasus-nunukan.

Hukum Online. 2006. "Citizen Law Suit Kasus Nunukan Kalah di Tingkat Banding," November 27. Accessed July 6, 2016, http://www.hukumonline.com/berita /baca/hol15797/citizen-law-suit-kasus-nunukan-kalah-di-tingkat-banding.

INFID, ed. 1993. *Pembangunan di Indonesia: Memandang Dari Sisi Lain*. Jakarta: Yayasan Obor and INFID.

Institute for Ecosoc Rights. n.d. "What Do We Work On?" Accessed May 9, 2016, http://ecosocrights.blogspot.com.au/2006/04/what-do-we-work-on.html.

International Development Law Organization. 2010. *10 Reasons Why Legal Services Must Be Central to a Rights-based Response to HIV*. Accessed January 14, 2016, http://www.idlo.org/Publications/10reasonsWhyHIV.pdf.

International Organization for Migration. 2010. *Labour Migration from Indonesia: An Overview of Indonesian Migration to Selected Destinations in Asia and the Middle East*. Jakarta: IOM.

Jakarta Post. 2002a. "Govt Gives Aid for Illegals," August 10.

Jakarta Post. 2002b. "Nunukan Remains 'Humanitarian Emergency,'" September 18.

Jakarta Post. 2005a. "Central Government Tells Sutiyoso to Bring Public Hospitals Back," March 2.

Jakarta Post. 2005b. "Sutiyoso Defends New Hospital Status," March 10.

Jakarta Post. 2005c. "VP, Sutiyoso Discuss Hospital Status," March 26.

Jakarta Post. 2006. "Supreme Court Nixes Corporatization of City-owned Hospitals," June 9.

Johar, M. 2009. "The Impact of the Indonesian Health Card Program: A Matching Estimator Approach," *Journal of Health Economics* 28:35–53.

Jong, H. 2015. "JKN Penalties Increased, Fees Raised," *The Jakarta Post*, July 2.

Khan, Irene, and David Petrasek. 2014. "Beyond the Courts—Protecting Economic and Social Rights." Accessed January 14, 2016, https://www.opendemocracy .net/openglobalrights/irene-khan-david-petrasek/beyond-courts-%e2%80%93 -protecting-economic-and-social-rights.

Kmiec, Keenan. 2004. "The Origin and Current Meanings of 'Judicial Activism,'" *California Law Review* 92 (5):1441–77.

Kompas. 2000. "Mendesak, Peningkatan Anggaran Kesehatan dan Pendidikan," January 28.

Kompas. 2003. "IDI Minta Parpol Prioritaskan Program Kesehatan," December 19.

Kompas. 2004a. "Info Jabotabek," June 22.

Kompas. 2004b. "Janji Yudhoyono Naikkan Persentase Anggaran Kesehatan," August 31.

Kompas. 2004c. "Privatisasi Ancam Akses Kesehatan Penduduk Miskin," December 17.

Kompas. 2004d. "Privatisasi Rumah Sakit Bukan Kebijakan Tepat," December 20.

Kompas. 2005a. "Sejumlah RSUD di Jakarta Menyusul Diswastakan," February 11.

Kompas. 2005b. "RSUD Diswastakan, Masyarakat Miskin Mati Pelan-Pelan," February 24.

Kompas. 2005c. "Puluhan Dokter RS Pasar Rebo Mogok, Pelayanan Pasien Terhambat," May 6.

Kompas. 2006a. "Kembalikan Status RSUD," June 9.

Kompas. 2006b. "Tiga RS DKI Batal Diswastakan," August 18.

Kuswardono Arif, Rusman, Darlis Muhamad, and Friets Kerlely. 2002. "Hari Kemenangan di Barak Pengungsian," *Tempo* December 8.

LBH Kesehatan. n.d. "Tentang Kami." Accessed August 2009, http://www.lbhkesehatan .org/Tentangkami.htm. URL no longer active; material available from Andrew Rosser.

Lindsey, Tim. 2008. "Constitutional Reform in Indonesia: Muddling Towards Democracy." In *Indonesia: Law and Society*, edited by Tim Lindsey, 23–47. Sydney: The Federation Press.

Liow, Joseph. 2003. "Malaysia's Illegal Indonesian Migrant Worker Labour Problem: In Search of Solutions," *Contemporary Southeast Asia* 25 (1):44–64.

Mahkamah Agung. 2005. *Putusan Nomor 05 P/Hum/Th.2005.*

Mahkamah Konstitusi. 2011a. *Putusan Nomor 50/PUU-VIII/2010.*

Mahkamah Konstitusi. 2011b. *Risalah Sidang Perkara Nomor 50/PUU-VIII/2010.*

Mahkamah Konstitusi. 2011c. *Putusan Nomor 60/PUU-IX/2011.*

Mahkamah Konstitusi. 2012. *Putusan Nomor 58/PUU-X/2012.*

McCann, Michael. 1994. *Rights at Work.* Chicago: University of Chicago Press.

Mietzner, Marcus. 2010. "Political Conflict Resolution and Democratic Consolidation in Indonesia: The Role of the Constitutional Court," *Journal of East Asian Studies* 10:397–424.

Miguel-Stearns, Teresa. 2015. "Judicial Power in Latin America: A Short Survey," *Legal Information Management* 15 (92):100–107.

Ministry of Finance. n.d. "APBN 2017." Accessed April 13, 2017, http://www.kemenkeu.go.id/apbn2017.

Ministry of Health. 2003. *Menyelamatkan Tenaga Kerja Indonesia (TKI) di Nunukan.* Jakarta: Ministry of Health.

Ministry of Health. 2014. *Indonesia Health Profile 2013.* Jakarta: Ministry of Health.

Murphy, Ann Marie. 2008. "The Role of Professional Organizations in Indonesia's Socio-Political Transformation," *NBR Analysis* 18 (3):17–34.

National Team for the Acceleration of Poverty Reduction. 2015. *The Road to National Health Insurance (JKN).* Jakarta: Office of the Vice President, The Republic of Indonesia.

Nunukan Humanitarian Tragedy Advocacy Team. 2003. *Gugatan Perbuatan Melawan Hukum atas Penanganan Buruh Migran Indonesia (TKI) Yang Dideportasi dari Malaysia di Nunukan.*

Pengadilan Negeri Jakarta Pusat. 2003. *Putusan Nomor 28/PDT.G/2003/PN.JKT.PST.*

Pengadilan Negeri Jakarta Pusat. 2011. *Putusan Nomor 278/ Pdt.G/ 2010/ PN.JKT.PST.*

Pengadilan Tinggi Jakarta. 2012. *Putusan Nomor 404/PDT/2012/PT.DKI.*

Pompe, Sebastian. 2005. *The Indonesian Supreme Court: A Study of Institutional Collapse.* Ithaca, NY: Cornell Southeast Asia Program.

Ramesh, M. 2014. "Social Protection in Indonesia and the Philippines: Work in Progress," *ASEAN Economic Bulletin* 31 (1):40–56.

Robison, Richard, and Vedi Hadiz. 2004. *Reorganising Power in Indonesia: The Politics of Oligarchy in an Age of Markets.* London: Routledge.

Rosenberg, Gerald. 1991. *The Hollow Hope: Can Courts Bring About Social Change?* Chicago: University of Chicago Press.

Rosser, Andrew. 2012. "Realising Free Health Care for the Poor in Indonesia: The Politics of Illegal Fees," *Journal of Contemporary Asia* 42 (2):255–75.

Rosser, Andrew. 2015a. "Contesting Tobacco Control Policy in Indonesia," *Critical Asian Studies* 47 (1):69–93.

Rosser, Andrew. 2015b. "Law and the Realisation of Human Rights: Insights from Indonesia's Education Sector," *Asian Studies Review* 39 (2):194–212.

Rosser, Andrew. 2016. "Neoliberalism and the Political Economy of Higher Education Policy in Indonesia," *Comparative Education* 52 (2):109–35.

Rosser, Andrew, and Jayne Curnow. 2014. "Legal Mobilisation and Justice: Insights from the Constitutional Court Case on International Standard Schools in Indonesia," *The Asia-Pacific Journal of Anthropology* 15 (4):302–18.

Rosser, Andrew, and Maryke van Diermen. 2016. "Predation, Productivism, and Progressiveness: The Political Economy of Welfare Capitalism in Post–New Order Indonesia, *Asia Review* 5 (2):157–82.

Rosser, Andrew, Kurnya Roesad, and Donni Edwin. 2005. "Indonesia: The Politics of Inclusion," *Journal of Contemporary Asia* 35 (1):53–77.

Santosa, Mas Achmad. 2007. "Class Actions in Indonesia." Accessed December 12, 2016, http://globalclassactions.stanford.edu/content/class-actions-indonesia.

Scheingold, Stuart. 1974. *The Politics of Rights: Lawyers, Public Policy and Political Change.* New Haven, CT: Yale University Press.

Serikat Rakyat Miskin Indonesia. n.d. "Mengenal SRMI." Accessed July 8, 2016, http://dpn-srmi.blogspot.com.au/2009/11/srmi.html.

Singh, Jerome Amir, Michelle Govender, and Edward J. Mills. 2007. "Do Human Rights Matter to Health?," *The Lancet* 370 (August 11):521–27.

Sirait. 2004. "Lembaga Ini Tidak Akan Bisa Didikte," *Tabloid Reformata*, September.

Stalker, Peter. 2000. *Beyond Krismon: The Social Legacy of Indonesia's Financial Crisis.* Florence: UNICEF Innocenti Research Centre.

Sucipto, Yenny, Dani Setiawan, Abdul Wiadl, and Ah Maftuchan. 2015. *APBN Konstitutional: Prinsip dan Pilihan Kebijakan.* Yogyakarta: Galang.

Sujudi, Achmad et al. 2004. *Membangun Fondasi Reformasi Kesehatan: Rekaman Pembangunan Kesehatan Periode 1999–2004.* Jakarta: Ministry of Health.

Sulastomo. 1981. *Manajemen Kesehatan.* Jakarta: PT Gramedia Pustaka Utama.

Sumarto, Sudarno, and Samuel Bazzi. 2011. "Social Protection in Indonesia: Past Experiences and Lessons for the Future," paper presented at the 2011 Annual Bank Conference on Development Opportunities (ABCDE) jointly organized by the World Bank and OECD, May 30–June 1, 2011, Paris.

Supari, Siti Fadillah. 2010. "IDI Harus Mencegah Terjadinya Neo Liberalisasi Bidang Kesehatan di Indonesia." In *60 Tahun Ikatan Dokter Indonesia: Rekam Jejak, Pandangan dan Harapan,* edited by Daeng Faqih and Zaenal Abidin Jakarta, 302–09. Jakarta: Ikatan Dokter Indonesia.

Susanti, Bivitri. 2008. "The Implementation of the Rights to Health Care and Education in Indonesia." In *Courting Social Justice: Judicial Enforcement of Social and Economic Rights in the Developing World,* edited by Varun Gauri and Daniel Brinks, 224–67. New York: Cambridge University Press.

Tahyar, Benjamin. 2012. "Patrimonialism, Power and the Politics of Judicial Reform in Post-Soeharto Indonesia: An Institutional Analysis." Unpublished PhD dissertation, School of Oriental and African Studies.

Tans, R. 2011. "Mafias, Machines and Mobilization: The Sources of Local Power in Three Districts in North Sumatra, Indonesia." Unpublished MA thesis, National University of Singapore.

Taylor-Nicholson, Eleanor. 2013. "Menciptakan Kerangka Kerja Buruh Migran yang Lebih Kuat untuk Dekade Berikutnya," Yayasan TIFA/UNSW Law Policy Brief, October.

Tempo Interaktif. 2005a. "Presiden Tidak Setuju Privatisasi Rumah Sakit Milik Pemerintah," February 25.

Tempo Interaktif. 2005b. "Dokter Mogok Karena Solidaritas," May 5. Accessed November 8, 2014, http://tempo.co.id/hg/jakarta/2005/05/05/brk,20050505-17, id.html. URL no longer active; material available from Andrew Rosser.

Tempo Interaktif. 2005c. "Depkes Tolak Privatisasi Rumah Sakit," May 26. Accessed November 5, 2014, http://www.tempo.co/read/news/2005/05/26/05561482/Depkes-Tolak-Privatisasi-Rumah-Sakit. URL no longer active; material available from Andrew Rosser.

Tempo.co. 2016. "Oktober 2016 Jumlah Peserta JKN 169,5 Juta Jiwa," October 24. Accessed February 2, 2017, https://m.tempo.co/read/news/2016/10/24/060814749/oktober-2016-jumlah-peserta-jkn-169-5-juta-jiwa. URL no longer active; material available from Andrew Rosser.

Thabrany, Hasbullah. 2005. "Rumah Sakit Publik Berbentuk BLU: Bentuk Paling Pas Dalam Koridor Hukum Saat Ini," paper presented at a seminar on Kontroversi Pengelolaan dan Bentuk Kelembagaan Rumah Sakit Pemerintah, Jakarta, March 12.

Thabrany, Hasbullah, Ascobat Gani, Pujianto, Laura Mayanda, Mahlil, and Bagus Satria Budi. 2003. "Social Health Insurance in Indonesia: Current Status and the Plan for a National Health Insurance," paper presented at the WHO SEARO workshop on Social Health Insurance, New Delhi, March 13–15.

Thompson, David. 2015. "The Surprising Role of the Judiciary in Health Care Decision Making in Latin America: Insights From Local Experts," *ISPOR News*, March/April:28–30.

Thompson, Geoff. 2008. "US Involved in Bird Flu Conspiracy," Australian Broadcasting Corporation's AM program. Accessed March 13, 2016, http://www.abc.net.au/am/content/2008/s2167325.htm.

Tjandra, Surya. 2014. "The Indonesian Trade Union Movement under Reformasi," unpublished paper.

Topatimasang, Roem, Wilarsa Budiharga, Toto Rahardjo, Ahmad Mahmudi, Yoga Atmaja, Handoko Soetomo, Ayi Bunyamin, Hambali, Mardiati Nadjib, Prastuti Chusnun, Mahlil Rubi, Laura Mayanda, Ede Darmawan, Donatus Marut, and Etik Wati. 2005. *Sehat Itu Hak: Panduan Advokasi Masalah Kesehatan Masyarakat*, Jakarta and Yogyakarta: Koalisi Untuk Indonesia Sehat and INSIST.

Trisnantoro, Laksono, ed. 2003. *Desentralisasi Kesehatan di Indonesia dan Perubahan Fungsi Pemerintah: 2001–2003: Apakah Merupakan Periode Uji Coba?* Yogyakarta: Gadjah Mada University Press.

Trisnantoro, Laksono. 2010. "Ideologi Apa yang Dianut Oleh Kebijakan Kesehatan di Indonesia," *Jurnal Manajemen Pelayanan Kesehatan* 13 (4):167–68.

Triwibowo, Darmawan, and Sugeng Bahagijo. 2006. *Mimpi Negara Kesejahteraan*, Jakarta: LP3ES and Perkumpulan Prakarsa.

UNICEF Indonesia. 2012. *Responding to HIV and AIDS*, Unicef Issue Brief. Accessed November 29, 2016, https://www.unicef.org/indonesia/A4-_E_Issue_Brief_HIV_REV.pdf.

United Nations Committee on Economic, Social and Cultural Rights. 2000. *General Comment 14: The Right to the Highest Attainable Standard of Health (Art. 12)*.

Vivanews. 2009. "Golkar Janjikan Anggaran Kesehatan 5% APBN," February 3. Accessed June 23, 2016, http://www.viva.co.id/berita/politik/26722-golkar -janjikan-anggaran-kesehatan-5-apbn

Wilson, Bruce. 2011. "Costa Rica: Health Rights Litigation: Causes and Consequences." In *Litigating Health Rights: Can Courts Bring More Justice to Health?*, edited by Alicia Yamin and Siri Gloppen, 132–54. Cambridge, MA: Harvard University Press.

Wisnu, Dinna. 2012. *Politik Sistem Jaminan Sosial: Menciptakan Rasa Aman Dalam Ekonomi Pasar.* Jakarta: PT Gramedia Pustaka Utama.

Witoelar, W. 2000. "Firman Lubis: Kesehatan Juga Perlu Mengalami Reformasi." Accessed May 8, 2016, http://www.perspektifbaru.com/wawancara/242.

World Bank. 2008. *Investing in Indonesia's Health: Challenges and Opportunities for Future Public Spending.* Jakarta: World Bank.

World Bank. 2009a. *Giving More Weight to Health: Assessing Fiscal Space for Health in Indonesia.* Jakarta: World Bank.

World Bank. 2009b. *Indonesia Health Sector Review: Pharmaceuticals: Why Reform Is Needed.* Jakarta: World Bank.

Yamin, Alicia. 2014. "Promoting Equity in Health: What Role for Courts?," *Health and Human Rights Journal* 16 (2):1–9.

Yamin, Alicia, and Siri Gloppen, eds. 2011. *Litigating Health Rights: Can Courts Bring More Justice to Health?* Cambridge, MA: Harvard University Press.

Young, Katherine, and Julieta Lemaitre. 2013. "The Comparative Fortunes of the Right to Health: Two Tales of Justiciability in Colombia and South Africa." *Harvard Human Rights Journal* 26:179–216.

Acknowledgments

I wish to thank Marcus Mietzner, Maryke van Diermen, and two anonymous reviewers for their helpful comments on earlier drafts of this study. Any errors remaining are the responsibility of the author. I also wish to thank the Australian Research Council for supporting this research under grant number FT110100078.

www.ingramcontent.com/pod-product-compliance
Lightning Source LLC
Chambersburg PA
CBHW051504270326
41933CB00021BA/3463